good food eat well

SPIRALIZER RECIPES

Editor **Sophie Godwin**

D0048638

BOOKS

Contents
. . . .

Introduction

You may have been bought a spiralizer for Christmas or are thinking of purchasing one but are not sure what to do with it aside from spiralizing courgette. We've come up with a collection of simple recipes to help you get the most out of spiralizing.

From a chapter on sides, snacks and canapés with exciting new ideas that are sure to impress your friends to our family favourites section with healthier remakes of much-loved classics that the whole family are sure to enjoy.

If you are a pasta lover then our swap the carbs chapter is for you, with loads of delicious recipes using vegetable alternatives. Butternut mac n cheese anyone?

My favourite collection is the salad recipes that are full of flavour, vibrant and colourful.

Whether you're in need of a bowl of nourishment and comfort or a light and refreshing gazpacho, our soups and stews chapter have got it covered with plenty of original recipes showcasing fruit and vegetables.

We've also included some delicious recipes that help you get the most out of your vegetables, whether that be in a cauliflower pizza, a pastry-less pie or a soup that uses up a bag of mixed salad leaves, all our recipes will put you on your way to reaching your five-a-day.

As always, all of the recipes in this book have been tested in the BBC Good Food kitchen, so you can rest safe in the knowledge that they will work first and every time for you, too.

Sophie Godwin, Cookery Writer
BBC Good Food magazine

Notes &
conversion tables
· · · · · · · · · · · · · · · · · · · ·

- Eggs are large in the UK and Australia and extra large in America unless stated.
- Wash fresh produce before preparation.
- Recipes contain nutritional analyses for 'sugars', which means the total sugar content including all natural sugars in the ingredients, unless otherwise stated.

OVEN TEMPERATURES

GAS	°C	°C FAN	°F	OVEN TEMP.
¼	110	90	225	Very cool
½	120	100	250	Very cool
1	140	120	275	Cool or slow
2	150	130	300	Cool or slow
3	160	140	325	Warm
4	180	160	350	Moderate
5	190	170	375	Moderately hot
6	200	180	400	Fairly hot
7	220	200	425	Hot
8	230	210	450	Very hot
9	240	220	475	Very hot

APPROXIMATE WEIGHT CONVERSIONS
- All the recipes in this book use metric measurements. Conversions are approximate and have been rounded up or down. Follow one set of measurements only; do not mix the two.
- Cup measurements, which are used in Australia and America, have not been listed here as they vary from ingredient to ingredient. Kitchen scales should be used to measure dry/solid ingredients.

Good Food is concerned about sustainable sourcing and animal welfare. Where possible, humanely reared meats, sustainably caught fish (see fishonline.org for further information from the Marine Conservation Society) and free-range chickens and eggs are used when recipes are originally tested.

SPOON MEASURES

Spoon measurements are level unless otherwise specified.

- 1 teaspoon (tsp) = 5ml
- 1 tablespoon (tbsp) = 15ml
- 1 Australian tablespoon = 20ml (cooks in Australia should measure 3 teaspoons where 1 tablespoon is specified in a recipe)

APPROXIMATE LIQUID CONVERSIONS

METRIC	IMPERIAL	AUS	US
50ml	2fl oz	¼ cup	¼ cup
125ml	4fl oz	½ cup	½ cup
175ml	6fl oz	¾ cup	¾ cup
225ml	8fl oz	1 cup	1 cup
300ml	10fl oz/½ pint	½ pint	1¼ cups
450ml	16fl oz	2 cups	2 cups/1 pint
600ml	20fl oz/1 pint	1 pint	2½ cups
1 litre	35fl oz/1¾ pints	1¾ pints	1 quart

Mini butternut squash frittatas

Great for kids and adults alike. Make a batch of these at the weekend and add them to your lunchbox for a tasty snack.

🕐 TAKES 50 mins   🍴 SERVES 12

- 1 tbsp olive oil, plus extra for greasing
- 1 large butternut squash (about 1.4kg) peeled, ends trimmed, halved widthways and spiralized into thin noodles
- 1 red onion, ends trimmed, peeled and spiralized into flat noodles
- 1 red chilli, finely chopped and deseeded, if you like
- 6 large eggs
- 4 sprigs thyme, leaves picked
- 100g goat's cheese, broken into pieces

1 Heat oven to 180C/160C fan/gas 4. Lightly oil 12 holes of a muffin tin.

2 Pull apart any squash spirals that are stuck together and cut any long spirals of squash in half. Heat the oil in a frying pan over a medium heat then add the spiralized squash and red onion. Cook, stirring occasionally for 3 mins until the vegetables have softened slightly. Stir in the red chilli, fry for a further min then remove from the heat and allow to cool slightly.

3 Beat the eggs in a large jug or bowl and season with salt and a generous grind of black pepper. Stir in the butternut squash mixture along with the thyme leaves and goat's cheese.

4 Divide the mixture between each muffin tin, making sure each hole gets an equal amount of filling, then bake in the oven for 15–18 mins or until just set. Gently lift the fritattas out of the tin with a palette or cutlery knife.

1 PER SERVING 96 kcals, fat 5g, sat fat 2g, carbs 6g, sugars 3g, fibre 1g, protein 6g, salt 0.2g

Beetroot & avocado nori rolls with wasabi dipping sauce

The dipping sauce adds real punch to this vegan canapé, if you can't get hold of wasabi, substitute horseradish instead.

🕐 TAKES 40 mins   🍳 SERVES 15

FOR THE DIPPING SAUCE
- 1 tsp wasabi
- juice of ½ lime
- 2 tbsp dark soy sauce or tamari
- 1 tsp sesame oil

FOR THE NORI ROLLS
- 1 beetroot (about 120g) peeled, ends trimmed and spiralized into thin noodles
- 3 sheets of nori
- 1 ripe avocado, thinly sliced
- ½ cucumber, ends trimmed, cut in half widthways and spiralized into thin noodles then patted dry to absorb excess moisture
- 2 tsp toasted sesame seeds

1 Mix all of the ingredients for the dipping sauce together in a small bowl then set aside.

2 Cut the spiralized beetroot into thumb-length strips. Lay a nori sheet, shiny side down, onto a sushi rolling mat. Arrange one third of the beetroot, avocado and cucumber in lines across the bottom third of the nori sheet then sprinkle over half the sesame seeds.

3 Rolling away from yourself, lift the edge of the nori over the filling and continue folding to create a roll. When you get to the edge of the nori, dampen with a little water then continue to fold, sealing everything together into a tight roll.

4 Repeat with the remaining nori and filling. Trim the ends of the roll to neaten them then slice into 5 pieces. Serve with the wasabi dipping sauce.

PER SERVING 32 kcals, protein 1g, carbs 1g, fat 2g, sat fat 1g, fibre 1g, sugars 1g, salt 0.3g

Spiced kale crisps

· ·

Using this as a base recipe why not play around with different spices such as smoked paprika to flavour the kale chips.

🕐 TAKES 25 mins   🍴 SERVES 4-6

- 100g chunky chopped kale, or kale leaves, tough stalks removed (weight without stalks)
- ½ tbsp olive oil
- 1 heaped tsp ras el hanout

1 Heat oven to 150C/130C fan/gas 2 and line two baking trays with baking parchment. Wash the kale and dry thoroughly. Place in a large bowl, tearing any large leaves into smaller pieces. Drizzle over the oil, then massage into the kale. Sprinkle over the ras el hanout and some sea salt, mix well, then tip onto the trays and spread out in a single layer. Bake for 18–22 mins or until crisp but still green, then leave to cool for a few mins.

· ·

PER SERVING (6) 22 kcals, fat 1g, sat fat 0g, carbs 2g, sugars 0g, fibre 0g, protein 1g, salt 0.1g

Lime, sesame & coconut courgette carpaccio

. . . .

The freshness of this carpaccio is the ideal counterpart for a spicy dish. Try eating this with curry or sticky ribs.

🕐 TAKES 20 mins   🕐 SERVES 4

- 100g frozen shelled edamame beans
- 2 tbsp sesame oil
- juice of 1 lime
- 3 courgettes, ends trimmed and spiralized into thin noodles
- 150g pack mixed radishes, cut into wedges
- 3 tbsp flaked coconut, toasted

1 Bring a small saucepan of salted water to the boil. Drop in the edamame beans and cook for 3–4 mins then using a slotted spoon plunge into a bowl of ice-cold water. Once completely cool, tip into a sieve and leave to drain.

2 Mix the sesame oil with the lime juice in a small bowl with a little sea salt. Lay the courgette ribbons on a sharing platter. Scatter over the mixed radishes and edamame beans then drizzle over the dressing and top with the toasted coconut.

. . . .
PER SERVING 180 kcals, fat 14g, sat fat 7g, carbs 5g, sugars 4g, fibre 5g, protein 6g, salt 0g

Ham & mushroom potato nests with fried quail's eggs

· ·

Brunch with a difference! Bake the nests ahead of time then crack in the eggs and cook when your guests arrive.

🕐 TAKES 55 mins   🕒 SERVES 12

- 10g butter, plus extra for greasing
- 200g chestnut mushrooms, sliced
- 2 garlic cloves, crushed
- 500g waxy potatoes, peeled, ends trimmed and spiralized into thin noodles
- 120g pack of ham, torn into pieces
- 125g ball mozzarella, drained and grated
- 12 quail's eggs

1 Heat oven to 180C/160C fan/gas 4. Generously grease 12 holes of a non-stick muffin (or cupcake) tin with butter.

2 Heat the butter in a frying pan over a medium to high heat. Add the mushrooms. Fry for 4–5 mins until they begin to brown. Stir in the garlic, cook for 1 minute, then tip the mushrooms into a large bowl. Stir in the potato, ham and mozzarella. Season with salt and pepper.

3 Divide the mixture among the muffin holes and bake in the oven for 25 mins or until golden brown. Remove from the oven and run a cutlery or palette knife around the edges of the nests to make sure they are not sticking to the pan. Then use the back of a teaspoon to press down the centre of each to make an indent large enough to hold a quail egg. Crack a quail's egg into each nest and return to the oven for 8–10 mins, until the egg white is set and the yolk runny. Cool in the tin for 1-2 mins, then carefully lift out with a palette knife.

· ·
1 PER SERVING 108 kcals, fat 4g, sat fat 2g, carbs 9g, sugars 1g, fibre 1g, protein 7g, salt 0.4g

Baked carrot & nigella seed bhajis with raita

· ·

A good-for-you baked alternative to the much-loved bhaji. Serve as part of a thali.

🕐 TAKES 55 mins   🥮 SERVES 12

- 100g gram (chickpea) flour
- 1 tsp ground turmeric
- 2 tsp nigella seeds
- ½ tsp ground cumin, coriander, ginger and chilli powder
- 2 large eggs
- 4 large carrots (about 400g), peeled, ends trimmed and spiralized into thin noodles
- 2 tsp vegetable oil

FOR THE RAITA
- ½ cucumber, grated
- 150g pot of natural yoghurt
- ½ small pack of mint, leaves finely chopped

1 Heat oven to 200C/180C fan/gas 6. Line one large or two medium baking trays with baking parchment.
2 Mix all the ingredients for the carrot bhajis, apart from the carrot and oil, together in a large bowl to form a thick batter. If the mixture looks a little dry add a splash of water. Stir in the sprialized carrots, cutting any large spirals in half, and season.
3 Dollop 12 spoonfuls of the mixture onto the baking tray, leaving enough space to flatten the bhajis with the back of a spoon. Drizzle over the oil and bake for 25 mins or until golden brown, flipping the bhajis halfway.
4 While the bhajis are cooking, squeeze any excess moisture from the cucumber using a tea towel then combine all the ingredients for the raita together in a small bowl, seasoning to taste. Serve alongside the baked bhajis.

· · · · · · · · · · · · · · · · · · · ·
1 PER SERVING 70 kcals, fat 3g, sat fat 1g, carbs 7g, sugars 2g, fibre 2g, protein 4g, salt 0.1g

Quick pickled cucumber

These pickled cucumber ribbons are delicious with any smoked fish, particularly salmon.

🕐 TAKES 30 mins   🖐 SERVES 2

- 1 large cucumber, ends trimmed, cut in half widthways and spiralized into thick ribbons
- 1 tsp flaky sea salt
- 1 tbsp white wine vinegar
- 1 tbsp caster sugar
- ½ tsp coriander seeds
- a small handful of dill, leaves picked

1 Toss the cucumber ribbons with the salt in a colander. Leave for 15 mins then squeeze out any excess moisture with your hands and pat the ribbons dry with a tea towel.
2 Mix the other ingredients together in a small bowl then stir in the cucumber.

Dukkah-crusted squash wedges

Wedges get a Middle Eastern twist, roasted with home made-dukkah.

🕐 TAKES 45 mins 🍴 SERVES 4

- 50g blanched hazelnuts
- 1 tbsp coriander seeds
- 2 tbsp sesame seeds
- 1 tbsp ground cumin
- 1 large butternut squash, peeled, seeds removed and sliced into wedges
- 1 tbsp olive oil

1 Heat oven to 200C/180C fan/gas 6. Toast the hazelnuts in a frying pan over a medium heat until golden. Add the coriander and sesame seeds, and toast for 1 min more. Set aside and leave to cool, then add the ground cumin and bash together using a pestle and mortar.

2 Toss the butternut squash wedges with the oil in a large bowl, then mix in the dukkah coating. Spread in a single layer on a baking tray and cook for 30–40 mins, turning halfway through, until tender.

Roasted beets, plum & pecan salad

The earthiness of beetroot complements the sweet yet tart plums and toasted nuts in this side salad. Pair with lamb for an autumnal feast.

🕐 TAKES 30 mins   📐 SERVES 3-4 as a side

- 4 large raw beetroot (about 500g), peeled, ends trimmed and spiralized into thick noodles
- 1 tbsp olive oil
- 4 ripe plums (about 200g), cut into wedges
- 60g pecans, toasted and roughly chopped
- 1 small pack mint, leaves picked, some reserved for garnish

FOR THE DRESSING
- 1½ tbsp extra virgin olive oil ½ tbsp red wine vinegar
- ½ tbsp pomegranate molasses

1 Heat oven to 200C/180C fan/gas 6. Toss the spiralized beetroot in the olive oil and some seasoning in a roasting tin then spread out into an even layer. Roast for 15 mins until tender.

2 While the beetroot is roasting, combine the dressing ingredients together in a jug with a little seasoning.

3 To assemble the salad, toss the rest of the ingredients in the roasting tin with the cooked beetroot and dressing. Serve on a sharing platter, garnished with a few reserved mint leaves.

PER SERVING 246 kcals, fat 18g, sat fat 2g, carbs 14g, sugars 13g, fibre 6g, protein 4g, salt 0.2g

Skinny carrot fries

Tossed in tarragon, these skinny fries are a chip-lover's healthy alternative.

🕐 TAKES 55 mins   🍳 SERVES 2

- 500g carrots, cut into thick 'fries'
- 1 tbsp cornflour
- 1 tbsp vegetable oil
- 1 tsp tarragon, finely chopped

1 Heat oven to 200C/180C fan/gas 6. Toss the carrots in the cornflour, oil and a little black pepper. Spread in a single layer on a baking tray lined with parchment, and bake for 40–45 mins, turning halfway. Mix a little salt with the tarragon and toss through the cooked fries.

PER SERVING 164 kcals, fat 6g, sat fat 1g, carbs 25g, sugars 18g, fibre 8g, protein 2g, salt 0.4g

Courgetti fritters with tomato salsa

· ·

Swap chips and dips for these cumin-spiced fritters and zesty tomato salsa.

🕐 TAKES 35 mins 🍽 SERVES 6

FOR THE SALSA

- 300g pack of room-temperature, ripe vine cherry tomatoes, chopped
- 1 small pack of coriander, leaves and stalks chopped, (save stalks for the fritters)
- zest and juice of 1 lime (save zest for the fritters)
- 1 green chilli, finely chopped, deseeded, if you like
- 1 garlic clove, crushed
- 2 tbsp extra virgin olive oil

FOR THE FRITTERS

- 3 courgettes (about 500g), ends trimmed and spiralized into thin noodles
- 3 spring onions, thinly sliced
- 1 tsp ground cumin
- 100g self-raising flour
- 1 large egg, beaten
- 2 tbsp olive oil, for frying

1 Combine all the salsa ingredients together in a bowl and season with salt and pepper then set aside to let the flavour develop.

2 In a separate large bowl, mix together the spiralized courgette, coriander stalks, lime zest, cumin and flour (you may need to cut some of the longer courgetti in half). Stir in the beaten egg and season with salt and black pepper.

3 Working in 2 batches, heat half the oil in a non-stick frying pan over a medium heat. Shape the fritters with your hand then fry for 2–3 mins on each side until golden. Serve warm with the tomato salsa.

· ·

PER SERVING 168 kcals, fat 9g, sat fat 1g, carbs 16g, sugars 3g, fibre 3g, protein 5g, salt 0.2g

Butternut & harissa houmous

Houmous but not as you know it. Roasted squash, garlic and harissa give this dip a colourful twist.

🕒 TAKES 55 mins 📋 SERVES 6

- ½ butternut squash (about 400g), peeled and cut into chunks
- 3 garlic cloves, unpeeled
- 2 tbsp olive oil
- 3 tbsp tahini paste
- 1 tbsp harissa, plus a little extra for drizzling
- 400g can chickpeas, drained and rinsed

1 Heat oven to 200C/180C fan/gas 6. Put the butternut squash and garlic cloves in a roasting tin, season well and add 100ml water. Cover the tin with foil and bake for 45 mins, until the squash is really tender. Leave to cool.

2 Tip the squash into a food processor with any juices from the tin. Add the garlic cloves, squeezed out of their skins. Add the remaining ingredients, season with salt and blend to a paste.

3 Scrape the houmous into a bowl. Drizzle with extra harissa before serving.

PER SERVING 155 kcals, fat 9g, sat fat 1g, carbs 13g, sugars 3g, fibre 3g, protein 4g, salt 0.4g

Vietnamese prawn spiralized rolls

Spiralized carrot and courgette add colour and crunch to Vietnamese rolls.

🕐 TAKES 40 mins 🕐 SERVES 12

FOR THE DIPPING SAUCE
- juice of ½ lime
- 2 tbsp rice wine vinegar
- 1 tbsp palm sugar
- 3 tbsp fish sauce
- 1 red birds eye chilli, finely chopped (optional)

FOR THE ROLLS
- 6 rice paper wrappers
- ½ small pack mint, leaves picked
- ½ small pack coriander, leaves picked
- 12 large king prawns (about 100g)
- 1 large carrot (about 130g), ends trimmed and spiralized into thin noodles
- 1 courgette, ends trimmed and spiralized into thin noodles

1 Mix all the ingredients for the dipping sauce along with 50ml water in a bowl and set aside to allow the sugar to dissolve and flavour to infuse.
2 To assemble the rolls, fill a wide bowl with warm water and grab a clean damp tea towel to work on. Dip a rice paper wrapper into the water for a few seconds until it softens then carefully place onto the tea towel.
3 Put a few mint and coriander leaves in the centre of the wrapper then top with two prawns and a small handful of the spiralized veg, which may need to be cut up if the spirals are too long.
4 Fold the sides of the wrapper into the centre, over the filling, then fold in the edges, so that the filling is completely encased, then tightly roll. Repeat until all of the wrappers and filling have been used. To serve, slice on a diagonal and eat with the dipping sauce.

PER SERVING 41 kcals, fat 0.3g, sat fat 0.1g, carbs 7g, sugars 2g, fibre 1g, protein 3g, salt 0.9g

Roasted squash & red onion with pistachios

Showcase butternut squash with this vibrant vegan side. Works well as part of a mezze.

🕐 TAKES 40 mins   👐 SERVES 4

- 1 large butternut squash, peeled, ends trimmed, halved widthways and spiralized into thick noodles
- 1 large red onion, peeled, ends trimmed and spiralized using the ribbon attachment
- 2 tbsp olive oil
- 2 tsp sumac
- 50g pomegranate seeds
- 30g pistachios, toasted and roughly chopped

1 Heat oven to 200C/180C fan/gas 6. Toss the spiralized butternut squash and onion together with the oil, sumac, some sea salt and black pepper in a roasting tray. Spread out then roast for 25 mins until the vegetables are completely tender and beginning to caramelize.

2 Divide between plates and top with the pomegranate seeds and toasted pistachios.

PER SERVING 197 kcals, fat 9g, sat fat 1g, carbs 21g, sugars 13g, fibre 6g, protein 4g, salt 0g

Courgette ribbon salad

This zingy, raw salad is delicious alongside grilled fish and chicken.

🕐 TAKES 20 mins 🥧 SERVES 4

- juice 1 lemon
- 2 tbsp olive oil
- ½ small pack chives, chopped
- ½ small pack mint, chopped
- 300g courgettes, ends trimmed and spiralized into thick noodles

1 In a large bowl, pour in the lemon juice and season well with salt and pepper. Whisk in the olive oil then add the chopped herbs.
2 Put your spiralized cougette into the bowl with the dressing. Toss everything together and serve immediately.

Smoked mackerel & horseradish on baked beetroot rostis

A twist on a classic, these beetroot canapés make a great nibble with an aperitif.

🕐 TAKES 45 mins 🍳 SERVES 20

- 2 large beetroot (about 300g), peeled, ends trimmed and spiralized into thin noodles
- 2 medium Maris Piper potatoes (about 300g), peeled, ends trimmed and spiralized into thin noodles
- 1½ tbsp olive oil
- 150g smoked mackerel, skin removed and broken into 20 large flakes
- handful of chives, finely chopped

FOR THE HORSERADISH CRÈME FRAICHE
- 150g crème fraiche
- 1 tbsp hot horseradish sauce
- zest and juice of ½ lemon

1 Heat oven to 200C/180C fan/gas 6. Line two baking trays with baking parchment. Pat the spiralized vegetables dry with kitchen paper and cut any long spirals into shorter noodle lengths then tip into a large bowl with the olive oil and season with salt and pepper.

2 With your hands, shape the mixture into 20 small circles. Space out between the two baking trays, making sure there is enough space for each rosti to cook evenly. Bake for 20 mins or until firm and crisping at the edges, carefully flipping the rostis after 10 mins.

3 While the rostis are roasting, mix together the crème fraiche, horseradish, lemon zest and juice and a generous grind of black pepper together in a small bowl.

4 Top each rosti with a spoonful of horseradish crème fraiche, a piece of smoked mackerel and some chopped chives.

PER SERVING 81 kcals, fat 6g, sat fat 3g, carbs 5g, sugars 2g, fibre 1g, protein 2g, salt 0.2g

Courgetti with chilli, lemon, ricotta & mint

Use the best-quality ricotta you can find in this fresh and simple side.

TAKES 15 mins   SERVES 2

- 2 courgettes (about 400g), ends trimmed and spiralized into thin noodles
- ½ red chilli, thinly sliced,
- zest and juice of ½ lemon
- ½ small pack mint, leaves picked
- 50g soft ricotta

1 Toss the courgetti in a bowl with the chilli, lemon juice, ¾ of the mint, some flaky sea salt and black pepper. Put onto a plate and garnish with the lemon zest, reserved mint and top with the ricotta.

PER SERVING 124 kcals, fat 4g, saturates 0g, carbs 17g, sugars 8g, fibre 3g, protein 5g, salt 1.9g

Sweet potato curly fries

The much-loved childhood classic reinvented with spiralized sweet potato.

🕐 TAKES 45 mins   🄻 SERVES 4

- 400g sweet potatoes, peeled, ends trimmed and spiralized into large noodles
- 2 tbsp olive oil
- 1 tsp black onion seeds and smoked paprika
- ½ tsp ground cumin and mustard powder
- ¼ tsp celery salt and chilli powder
- ½ tsp demerara sugar

1 Heat oven to 200C/180C fan/gas 6. Lay the noodles out on a large baking tray and drizzle with the olive oil, toss well to coat the noodles then space them out on the baking tray making sure they end up as a single layer.

2 Bake in the oven for 20–25 mins, tossing around in the tray halfway through cooking, until tender and starting to crisp up and char at the edges.

3 While the fries are baking, mix all of the seasoning ingredients together in a bowl and add ¼ tsp salt and black pepper. Stir well and set aside.

4 Once ready, evenly scatter the seasoning over the fries while they are still hot then transfer to a serving dish.

PER SERVING 185 kcals, fat 6g, sat fat 1g, carbs 27g, sugars 14g, fibre 4g, protein 2g, salt 0.8g

Cheat's duck, hoisin and cucumber lettuce cups

A quick and easy, low-fat alternative to duck pancakes.

🕐 TAKES 25 mins   🖐 SERVES 12

- 2 duck breasts (about 340g), skin and fat removed then each breast cut into 6 thin strips
- ½ tsp five spice
- 1 tbsp vegetable oil
- 50ml hoisin sauce
- 4 spring onions, thinly sliced on a diagonal
- ½ cucumber, ends trimmed, cut in half widthways, spiralized into thin noodles and squeezed dry to remove excess water
- 3 baby gem lettuces, leaves separated
- 1 tbsp sesame seeds

1 On the chopping board you used to slice the duck, toss the duck strips in the five spice and a generous pinch of flaky sea salt and black pepper.

2 Heat a wok or non-stick, large, high-sided frying pan over a high heat. Once really hot add the oil along with the seasoned strips of duck breast and stir-fry for 2 mins. Reduce the heat slightly and spoon in the hoisin sauce, toss everything together and stir-fry for another min until the duck is just cooked then remove from the heat.

3 Divide the spring onions, spiralized cucumber and hoisin duck between the lettuce leaves then top with a sprinkling of sesame seeds to serve.

PER SERVING 67 kcals, fat 2g, sat fat 0.3g, carbs 3g, sugars 2g, fibre 1g, protein 9g, salt 0.3g

Baba ganoush & crudités

· ·

Don't be scared to really burn the outside of the aubergines. The darker you take them, the smokier and tastier the dip.

🕐 TAKES 45 mins   🕐 SERVES 6

- 4 large aubergines (about 1.2kg), pricked all over with a fork
- zest and juice of 1 lemon
- 2 fat garlic cloves, chopped
- 3 tbsp tahini
- 4 tbsp extra virgin olive oil, plus a little extra for drizzling

FOR THE CRUDITÉS

- 4 large carrots, ends trimmed and spiralized into thick noodles
- 1 large cucumber, ends trimmed, spiralized into thick ribbons and patted dry to remove excess water
- 1 large courgette, ends trimmed and spiralized into thick noodles
- 150g pack mixed radishes, cut into random shapes

1 Cover the hob in tin foil for ease of cleaning then put each aubergine on a single gas hob and cook, turning occasionally with tongs until the aubergines are completely charred and collapsed, this will take 10–15 mins. Alternatively, heat the grill to its highest setting, lay the aubergines on a baking tray and cook, turning occasionally, for 30 mins to achieve the same effect. While the aubergine is cooking, prep the vegetables.

2 Allow the aubergines to cool slightly then scoop out the soft flesh into a colander. Leave to drain for 30 mins to remove any excess water then blitz the aubergine along with the other baba ganoush ingredients and some seasoning in a food processor to however smooth or chunky you like.

3 Spoon the dip into a bowl and serve in the centre of the vegetable crudités.

· ·

PER SERVING 218 kcals, fat 13g, sat fat 2g, carbs 13g, sugars 12g, fibre 11g, protein 5g, salt 0.1g

Cauliflower crust pizza

Whizzed-up cauliflower with ground almonds and oregano make this herby gluten free pizza base.

🕐 TAKES 1 hour   🥧 SERVES 4 (makes 1 large pizza)

FOR THE BASE
- 1 cauliflower, core removed and florets roughly chopped
- 100g ground almonds
- 2 eggs, beaten
- 1 tbsp dried oregano

FOR THE TOPPING
- ½ large aubergine, thinly sliced lengthways into long strips
- 2 tbsp olive oil, plus extra for greasing
- 1 small red onion, cut into 8 wedges
- 125g ball mozzarella, drained and patted dry
- 25g Parmesan (or vegetarian alternative), grated

FOR THE TOMATO SAUCE
- 227g can chopped tomatoes
- 1 tbsp tomato purée
- 1 garlic clove, crushed
- ½ small bunch basil, leaves picked

1 Heat oven to 200C/180C fan/gas 6. Grease and line a baking tray with parchment. Blitz the cauliflower in a food processor until finely chopped, transfer to a bowl, cover in cling film and microwave for 6 mins. Cool, then squeeze out as much liquid as you can. Stir in the base ingredients with plenty of seasoning. Spread the cauliflower out on the tray in a pizza shape. Bake for 15–18 mins until golden brown and starting to crisp at the edges, then set aside.

2 Heat a griddle pan. Brush the aubergine with a little oil. Season and cook, in batches, for 5–6 mins, turning once, until softened and charred. Transfer to a plate. Repeat with the onions.

3 Mix the tomato sauce ingredients together in a blender. Transfer to a small saucepan and cook gently for 8-10 mins until thick. Tear half the basil leaves and stir through the sauce.

4 Turn the oven up to 240C/220C fan/gas 8. Spread the tomato sauce over the base and top with the veg and cheeses. Return to the oven for 10-12 mins, then scatter with the remaining basil leaves.

PER SERVING 463 kcals, fat 33g, sat fat 9g, carbs 12g, sugars 10g, fibre 8g, protein 26g, salt 0.7g

Ginger & soy salmon en papillote

Steaming the salmon in a parcel, in its own marinade, keeps the fish juicy and full of flavour.

🕐 TAKES 40 mins 📊 SERVES 2

- 2 tbsp light soy sauce
- 1 tbsp rice wine vinegar
- thumb-sized piece of ginger, finely grated
- 1 garlic clove, finely grated
- 2 skinless salmon fillets (about 140g each)
- 1 courgette, ends trimmed and spiralized into thin noodles
- 1 carrot, peeled, ends trimmed and spiralized into thin noodles
- 2 bulbs of pak choi (about 200g), leaves separated
- 1 red chilli, thinly sliced, deseeded if you like
- Thai Jasmine rice, to serve (optional)

1 Heat oven to 180C/160C fan/gas 4. Before you prep the veg mix together the soy, vinegar, ginger, garlic and some black pepper in a bowl. Add the salmon fillets, cover and leave to marinate for 10 mins at room temperature or up to 2 hrs in the fridge.

2 Tear two large sheets of baking parchment, big enough to encase the fish and vegetables in and put onto a baking tray.

3 Divide the vegetables between the centre of the paper and top each with a marinated salmon fillet and the sliced chilli. Bring the sides of the parchment up over the salmon and pour half of the remaining marinade over each fillet then scrunch the paper tightly together to seal the fish in a parcel.

4 Roast for 20–25 mins, until the salmon is just cooked through and flakes into large pieces. Serve the fish in the parcel with some rice, if you like.

PER SERVING 391 kcals, fat 21g, sat fat 4g, carbs 9g, sugars 8g, fibre 4g, protein 39g, salt 1.6g

Black bean nachos

Bake your own paprika crisps from spiralized potato for home-made nachos topped with beans, cheese and roasted red pepper salsa.

🕐 TAKES 45 mins   🌡 SERVES 3-4

- 700g Maris Piper or King Edward potatoes, scrubbed, ends trimmed, spiralized using the straight blade into flat ribbons and then cut into round slices
- 2 tbsp olive oil
- 1 tsp smoked paprika
- 100g extra-mature Cheddar, grated
- 1 x 400g can of black beans, drained and washed
- ½ small pack coriander, roughly chopped

FOR THE ROASTED RED PEPPER SALSA

- 20g sliced pickled jalapeños, deseeded and chopped
- 100g roasted red peppers, chopped
- 1 small red onion, finely chopped
- 1 tbsp extra virgin olive oil

1 Heat the oven to 220C/200C fan/gas 8. Line two large or four medium baking sheets with baking parchment. Brush the potato slices with olive oil on both sides then transfer to the lined baking sheets, season with sea salt and black pepper then sprinkle over the paprika. Bake for 10–15 mins, until completely crisp. Check the crisps often as some will cook quicker than others. Remove those that are cooked and return any soft crisps back to the oven for another 2–3 mins.

2 Reduce the oven to 200C/180C fan/gas 6. Transfer half the crisps to a large ovenproof dish, layer with half the beans and half the cheese then repeat with the remaining ingredients. Return to the oven for 10 mins until the cheese has melted.

3 While the cheese is melting, mix all the ingredients for the salsa together in a small bowl, seasoning to taste. Top the nachos with dollops of the salsa (keeping the rest on the side) and chopped coriander.

PER SERVING (4) 384 kcals, fat 17g, sat fat 7g, carbs 38g, sugars 2g, fibre 8g, protein 14g, salt 1.2g

Ratatouille with poached eggs

Adding eggs to a classic ratatouille makes this one-pot a great dish for brunch and dinner.

⏱ TAKES 1 hour 5 mins   🍰 SERVES 4

- 1 tbsp olive oil
- 1 large onion, chopped
- 1 red or orange pepper, deseeded and thinly sliced
- 2 garlic cloves, finely chopped
- 1 tbsp rosemary, chopped
- 1 aubergine, diced
- 2 courgettes, diced
- 400g can chopped tomatoes
- 1 tsp balsamic vinegar
- 4 large eggs
- handful of basil leaves

1 Heat the oil in a large frying pan. Add the onion, pepper, garlic and rosemary, then cook for 5 mins, stirring frequently, until the onion has softened. Add the aubergine and courgettes, then cook for 2 mins more.

2 Add the tomatoes, then fill the can with water, swirl it around and tip into the pan. Bring to the boil, cover, then simmer for 40 mins, uncovering after 20 mins, until reduced and pulpy.

3 Stir the vinegar into the ratatouille, then make 4 spaces for the eggs. Crack an egg into each hole and season with black pepper. Cover, then cook for 2–5 mins until set as softly or firmly as you like then scatter over the basil.

PER SERVING 190 kcals, fat 11g, sat fat 2g, carbs 13g, sugars 10g, fibre 5g, protein 12g, salt 0.36g

Steak with rosemary celeriac fries, kale & garlic butter

Swap potato for celeriac for this healthier modern-day take on steak and chips.

🕐 TAKES 40 mins 🔋 SERVES 2

- ½ celeriac (about 350g), peeled, halved, ends trimmed and spiralized into thick noodles, then cut to be the size of fries
- 1 tbsp olive oil
- 2 sprigs of rosemary, leaves picked and finely chopped
- 2 sirloin steaks (about 200g each)
- 150g sliced kale

FOR THE HERBY GARLIC BUTTER
- 30g butter, softened at room temperature
- 1 garlic clove, crushed
- handful of parsley, finely chopped
- zest of ½ lemon

1 Heat oven to 200C/180C fan/gas 6. Mix the butter in a bowl with the garlic, parsley and lemon zest. Scrape out onto a piece of cling film, roll into a sausage and keep in the fridge until needed.

2 Toss the spiralized celeriac on a large baking tray in ½ tbsp oil, rosemary and some seasoning then spread out the celeriac, leaving enough room between the 'fries' that they cook evenly. Roast in the oven for 20 mins until tender and crisped.

3 Heat a large frying pan over a high heat while you season the steaks. Once searing hot add the remaining oil and the steaks. Cook for 2 mins on each side for medium rare, then set aside on a plate to rest.

4 While the steak is resting, put the kale in a large microwaveable bowl with 50ml water. Cover then cook on high for 3–4 mins, or until wilted. Slice the butter into rounds. Serve on top of the steak and kale alongside the celeriac fries.

PER SERVING 598 kcals, fat 40g, sat fat 17g, carbs 11g, sugars 3g, fibre 9g, protein 45g, salt 1g

Mushroom fajitas with avocado houmous

Get four out of your five-a-day with these simple grilled mushroom fajitas.

🕐 TAKES 35 mins   👐 SERVES 2

- 1 large avocado, stoned, peeled and chopped
- 400g can chickpeas, drained and rinsed
- 1 garlic clove, crushed
- zest and juice 1 lemon
- 2 tomatoes, deseeded and diced
- 1 red onion, cut into thick rounds
- 2 large flat mushrooms, thickly sliced
- 2 tbsp olive oil
- 2 tsp fajita spice mix
- 4 tortillas
- shredded Little Gem lettuce and Tabasco sauce, to serve (optional)

1 Put the avocado, chickpeas, garlic, lemon zest and juice in a food processor and whizz together until it forms a chunky consistency. Spoon into a bowl, season and stir in the tomatoes.

2 Drizzle the onion and mushrooms with the oil and sprinkle over the fajita seasoning. Heat a griddle pan over a high heat and cook the onion rounds for 2 mins on each side, then remove from the pan and keep warm. Cook the mushrooms for 2 mins on each side or until softened and turning golden in places.

3 Spread some of the avocado houmous down the middle of each wrap and top with the mushrooms and onions. Add shredded lettuce and a dash of Tabasco, if you like, and wrap up.

PER SERVING 824 kcals, fat 36g, sat fat 6g, carbs 104g, sugars 11g, fibre 14g, protein 23g, salt 2.3g

Thai red salmon curry

Turnip noodles make a delicious carb alternative for this Thai fish curry.

🕐 TAKES 45 mins   🍽 SERVES 2

- 1 tbsp groundnut oil
- 1 onion, ends trimmed and spiralized on the flat blade of the spiralizer
- ½ small pack coriander, stalks finely chopped and leaves picked
- 1 garlic clove, finely chopped
- thumb-sized piece of ginger, grated
- 2 tbsp Thai red curry paste
- 200ml coconut milk
- 150ml low-sodium veg stock
- 2 skinless, boneless salmon fillets, each cut into 4 large chunks
- 200g sugar snap peas
- 1 turnip (about 155g), peeled, ends trimmed and spiralized into the very thin noodles
- 1 lime, cut into wedges

1 Heat the oil in a sauté pan over a low to medium heat. Add the onion and cook gently for 8 mins until softened but not coloured. Stir in the coriander stalks, garlic and ginger. Cook for 1 min then increase the heat slightly, spoon in the curry paste and cook for a further min until smelling fragrant.

2 Pour in the coconut milk and veg stock, stir everything together and bring to the boil. Once boiling reduce the heat to a simmer, add the salmon chunks, sugar snap peas and spiralized turnip.

3 Simmer gently for 5 minutes until everything is nicely cooked, the salmon should come away in large flakes when pressed. Garnish with coriander leaves and lime wedges for serving.

PER SERVING 682 kcals, fat 49g, sat fat 20g, carbs 21g, sugars 13g, fibre 8g, protein 36g, salt 0.8g

Turkey, courgetti & feta burgers

Turkey mince, courgette, feta and mint give these burgers a healthy makeover.

🕐 TAKES 40 mins including chilling time   🍽 SERVES 4

- 500g lean turkey mince
- 100g feta, crumbled
- 1 large courgette (about 200g), ends trimmed, halved widthways and spiralized into thin noodles
- 2 garlic cloves, crushed
- ½ small pack mint, leaves picked and chopped
- ½ tsp chilli flakes
- 1 tsp sumac
- zest and juice of 1 lemon (save the juice for the salad)
- 1 large egg, beaten
- 1 tsp olive oil

FOR THE TOMATO SALAD
- 2 tbsp extra virgin olive oil•
  110g bag of rocket salad
- 250g pack cherry tomatoes, halved

1 Mix all of the ingredients for the turkey burgers, bar the olive oil, together in a large bowl. Season with a generous amount of black pepper and a little salt (you won't need a lot because of the feta). Shape into 4 burgers, the mixture will be quite sticky so cover and chill in the fridge for 15 mins or until needed to firm up a little. At this point the burgers can also be frozen.

2 Preheat the grill to its highest setting then brush the burgers on both sides with the olive oil. Transfer the burgers to a non-stick baking tray and cook for 8-10 mins on each side, until cooked through and golden brown.

3 While the burgers are cooking, mix together the olive oil, lemon juice and some seasoning. Add the rocket and tomatoes to a large salad bowl, add half the dressing and toss well to combine. Serve alongside the turkey burgers and with the extra dressing on the side.

PER SERVING 307 kcals, fat 14g, sat fat 5g, carbs 4g, sugars 3g, fibre 2g, protein 39g, salt 0.9g

Roasted squash, pancetta & chestnut risotto

Upping the veg and swapping rice for pearl barley makes a hearty winter warmer that is good for you.

🕐 TAKES 50 mins 📑 SERVES 3-4

- 1 large butternut squash (about 1.5kg), peeled, ends trimmed, cut in half widthways and spiralized into thin noodles
- 1½ tbsp olive oil
- 1 tsp chilli flakes
- 100g cooked chestnuts, quartered
- ½ small pack sage, leaves picked
- 8 slices pancetta
- 2 banana shallots, finely chopped
- 2 garlic cloves, finely chopped
- 200g pearl barley
- 850ml low-sodium vegetable stock (we used bouillon)
- Parmesan, to serve

1 Heat oven to 200C/180C fan/gas 6. Toss the squash with ½ tbsp of oil, chilli flakes and some seasoning on a large roasting tray. Roast for 15 mins, then add the chestnuts and nestle the sage and pancetta around the squash so that they touch the baking sheet. Return to the oven for 8–10 mins until the pancetta and sage are crisp. Remove from the oven and set aside. When cool, tear the pancetta and sage leaves into pieces.

2 Heat the remaining oil in a sauté pan over a low heat. Add the shallots and cook for 8 mins until softened but not coloured. Add the garlic and cook for 1 min. Tip in the pearl barley, toast for a minute, then pour in the stock.

3 Working in small amounts, add the stock to the pan and cook, stirring over a medium heat until all the liquid is absorbed by the barley – about 20 mins. When there is only a little liquid left, stir in the roasted ingredients to warm through. Season to taste. Serve with Parmesan.

PER SERVING (4) 418 kcals, fat 13g, sat fat 3g, carbs 62g, sugars 7g, fibre 4g, protein 11g, salt 0.7g

Mediterranean spelt-stuffed peppers

Olives, sundried tomatoes and basil pack a flavour punch in these stuffed peppers.

🕐 TAKES 45 mins 🕐 SERVES 4

- 4 large red peppers, halved and deseeded (stems left on)
- 100g fresh sundried (sometimes called semidried or sunblush) tomatoes, chopped plus 2 tbsp tomato oil
- 1 large red onion, ends trimmed and spiralized on the flat blade of the spiralizer
- 1 large courgette, halved widthways, ends trimmed and spiralized into thin noodles
- 250g pouch pre-cooked spelt
- 100g mixed olives, pips removed and chopped
- 1 small pack of basil, shredded
- green salad, to serve

1 Heat oven to 200C/180C fan/gas 6. Place the peppers cut side up on a roasting tray. Drizzle over 1 tbsp of the sundried tomato oil, season with sea salt and black pepper then roast for 20–25 mins until the peppers are tender.

2 Meanwhile, heat the remaining oil in a frying pan over a medium heat. Add the spiralized red onion. Cook for 2–3 mins until softened then transfer to a bowl.

3 Add in the remaining ingredients and some seasoning. Once the peppers are cooked, generously fill them with the spelt mix and return to the oven for 5 mins to heat through. Serve with a green salad.

PER SERVING 345 kcals, fat 11g, sat fat 2g, carbs 44g, sugars 22g, fibre 12g, protein 10g, salt 0.8g

Indian sweet potato & dhal pies

Warm and comforting pies that also count towards four of your five-a-day.

🕐 TAKES 40 mins   📂 SERVES 2

- 650g sweet potatoes, peeled and cut into small chunks
- generous tbsp 0% Greek-style yoghurt
- 2 tsp olive oil
- 1 large onion, thinly sliced
- 2 carrots, scrubbed, halved and sliced lengthways
- 2 garlic cloves, finely grated
- thumb-sized piece of ginger, finely grated
- 1 vegetable stock cube
- 2 tbsp tomato purée
- 85g red lentils
- good handful coriander, chopped
- broccoli, to serve (optional)

1 Cook the sweet potato in a pan of salted boiling water for 15 mins, or until tender, then drain and mash them with the yoghurt and seasoning.

2 Heat the oil in a pan and fry the onion and carrot for 2 mins over a high heat. Add the garlic and ginger and cook for a further minute. Tip in the curry powder then add 750ml of boiling water along with the stock cube, tomato purée and lentils. Cover the pan and boil for 20 mins until the veg is tender and the liquid has been absorbed. Stir in the coriander and heat the grill to its highest setting.

3 Spoon the lentil mix into one big or two individual dishes, then top with the sweet potato mixture. Put under the grill to brown a little, then serve with broccoli, if you like.

. . . .

PER SERVING 565 kcals, fat 4g, sat fat 1g, carbs 104g, sugars 41g, fibre 20g, protein 19g, salt 2.1g

Korean chicken wings with sesame slaw

Gochujang is a savoury spicy Korean condiment that adds a rich spiciness to these chicken wings.

🕐 TAKES 1 hour plus marinating   🕐 SERVES 4

- 2 tbsp gochujang sauce
- 2 tbsp honey
- 1 tbsp dark soy sauce
- juice of 2 limes, (1 in the marinade and the other in the slaw)
- 2 tsp sesame oil, (plus extra for drizzling in slaw)
- 1kg chicken wings

FOR THE SLAW
- 2 carrots, ends trimmed and spiralized into thin noodles
- 1 mooli (Daikon radish), ends trimmed and spiralized into thin noodles
- ½ red cabbage, shredded on the flat blade of the spiralizer
- 4 spring onions, thinly sliced on a diagonal
- 1½ tbsp black sesame seeds

1 In a large bowl, mix together the gochujang, honey, soy, juice of 1 lime and sesame oil. Toss in the chicken wings and leave to marinate for a couple of hours, or if you have time, overnight.

2 Heat oven to 200C/180C fan/gas 6. Transfer the wings to a large roasting tin, or two smaller ones, spreading out in a single layer so that they cook evenly. Roast for 50–55 mins, basting regularly until sticky and caramelized and the meat is starting to fall away from the bone.

3 While the wings are roasting, prepare the slaw. Mix all the ingredients together in a large bowl with a little sea salt and black pepper. Just before serving, drizzle over a little sesame oil and eat with the wings. Kitchen paper recommended.

PER SERVING 472 kcals, fat 24g, sat fat 6g, carbs 25g, sugars 22g, fibre 6g, protein 36g, salt 2.3g

Cider & mustard sausage wheel with box-grater salad

A colourful and modern take on bangers and mash.

🕐 TAKES 50 mins 🍴 SERVES 4

- 12 linked chipolatas
- drizzle of oil
- 250ml cider
- 2 tbsp wholegrain mustard, plus extra to serve (optional)
- 2 tbsp clear honey

FOR THE SALAD
- juice and zest 1 lemon
- 1 tbsp clear honey
- 1 tbsp extra virgin olive oil
- ½ small celeriac, peeled and grated
- 2 carrots and 2 raw beetroot, peeled and grated
- 1 apple, grated
- 100g mixed seeds (toasted if you have a spare pan)

1 Untwist the chipolata links and squeeze the meat along the sausage skin so that you have one long sausage. Roll the sausage into a cartwheel and push two wooden skewers through at right angles to secure. Heat a large frying pan with a drizzle of oil. Put the sausage wheel in the pan and cook over a medium heat for 8–10 mins until nicely browned on the underside. Flip over and cook for a further 8–10 mins until browned all over.

2 Whisk the cider, mustard and honey together until smooth, pour over the sausage and increase the heat. Bubble for 10–15 mins until reduced to a sticky glaze.

3 To make the salad, whisk the lemon juice and zest, honey and olive oil in a large bowl with some seasoning. Add the celeriac, carrot, beetroot, apple and mixed seeds and toss everything together. Cut the sausage into chunks and serve with the salad and some extra mustard, if you like.

PER SERVING 535 kcals, fat 32g, sat fat 8g, carbs 30g, sugars 25g, fibre 6g, protein 19g, salt 1.2g

Fish pie with shoestring potato topping

Using spiralized potato instead of mash gives the classic fish pie a crispy topping.

🕐 TAKES 45 mins   🥧 SERVES 4

- 200g frozen peas
- 3-4 large Maris Piper potatoes (about 600g) peeled, ends trimmed and spiralized into thin noodles
- 25g butter
- 25g flour
- 400ml milk
- zest and juice of 1 lemon, plus 1 lemon cut into wedges to serve
- 1 tsp Dijon mustard
- half a small pack of chives, chopped
- 100g asparagus tips, cut into thirds
- 300g skinless, boneless white fish cut into large chunks
- 150g pack raw king prawns
- 2 tbsp olive oil

1 Heat oven to 200C/180C fan/gas 6. Bring a large pan of salted water to the boil. Put the peas in a small sieve that will fit the pan. Lower and cook for 30 seconds, then lift out, run under cold water and leave to drain. Drop the potatoes into the boiling water and cook for 1 min to soften partially, then drain. Pat dry with kitchen paper and transfer to a separate bowl.

2 To make the white sauce, melt the butter in a large saucepan. Add the flour and cook for 1 min. Remove from the heat and slowly whisk in the milk until smooth then return to the heat, slowly bring up to the boil, whisking, then cook for 5–6 mins until you have a very thick sauce. Take off the heat and stir in the lemon zest and juice, mustard and chives. Gently stir in the peas, asparagus and fish.

3 Transfer the filling to an ovenproof dish. Toss the potato with the olive oil, some flaky sea salt and black pepper. Top the fish pie mix with the potato spirals and bake in the oven for 20–25 mins until hot through. For a crispy topping, put the pie under the grill for 5 mins until the potato is golden.

PER SERVING 436 kcals, fat 16g, sat fat 7g, carbs 40g, sugars 9g, fibre 6g, protein 30g, salt 0.7g

Beetroot falafel

Beetroot and tahini brighten up this Middle Eastern vegetarian favourite.

🕐 TAKES 55 mins ⏱ SERVES 6

- 1 tbsp olive oil
- 2 onions, chopped
- 2 tsp ground cumin
- 2 x 400g cans chickpeas, drained
- 500g raw beetroot, peeled, trimmed and coarsely grated
- 100g fresh breadcrumbs
- 1 egg
- 1 tbsp tahini paste
- vegetable oil, for brushing or frying

TO SERVE
- flatbreads
- 1 tbsp tahini mixed with 300ml natural yoghurt
- 1 bag of mixed salad leaves
- golden beetroot, diced (optional)

1 Heat the olive oil in a frying pan and fry the onions until softened but not coloured. Add the cumin and cook for 1 min, then scrape the mixture into a food processor with the chickpeas, two-thirds of the grated beetroot, the breadcrumbs, egg and tahini. Whizz to a rough paste, then scrape into a bowl and stir in the remaining grated beetroot with plenty of seasoning.

2 With damp hands, shape into about 20 balls and space on baking parchment-lined baking sheets. Chill until ready to cook.

3 Heat oven to 200C/180C fan/gas 6. Brush the falafels with a little vegetable oil and bake for 20–25 mins until crisp and hot through.

4 Serve the falafel in flatbreads with the tahini yoghurt and salad leaves topped with yellow beetroot, if you like.

PER SERVING 260 kcals, fat 7g, sat fat 1g, carbs 36g, sugars 8g, fibre 7g, protein 10g, salt 1.1g

Moroccan lamb kebabs

Coated in a Middle Eastern spice mix, these lamb kebabs are great cooked on the BBQ.

🕐 TAKES 35 mins plus marinating   🥧 SERVES 4

- 2 tsp ras el hanout
- 1 tbsp olive oil
- 4 lamb leg steaks (400g), trimmed of any fat and cut into about 24 equal-sized chunks
- 2 red peppers, deseeded and cut into chunks the same size as the lamb
- 2 large red onions, each cut into 8 wedges with the root attached
- 2 large courgettes, ends trimmed and spiralized into thin noodles
- 50g pine nuts, toasted
- juice of 1 lemon
- 1 small pack of parsley, chopped
- ½ tsp sweet paprika
- You will also need 8 skewers.

1 In a large bowl mix the ras el hanout with the oil then tip in the lamb, peppers and onions. Toss everything together and leave to marinate for at least half an hour, longer if time permits. If using wooden skewers soak them in warm water at this point to stop them burning.

2 Heat the grill to its highest setting. Season the marinated lamb mix then thread the lamb, alternating with the peppers and onions, onto the skewers and place on a non-stick baking tray. Cook for 8–10 mins until the lamb is tender, turning halfway.

3 While the lamb is grilling, mix together the courgetti, pine nuts, lemon juice, parsley and some seasoning. Divide between plates, top with the lamb kebabs then sprinkle over the sweet paprika.

PER SERVING 346 kcals, fat 18g, sat fat 4g, carbs 15g, sugars 13g, fibre 7g, protein 26g, salt 0.2g

Sweet potato hash with eggs & smashed avo

This sweet potato hash makes a great gluten-free brunch alternative to poached eggs and avocado on toast.

TAKES 30 mins   SERVES 2

- 1 large ripe avocado
- juice of 1 lime
- 1 tbsp olive oil
- 1 red onion, ends trimmed and spiralized on flat blade of the spiralizer
- 2 medium sweet potatoes (about 400g), ends trimmed and spiralized into thin noodles
- 2 large eggs
- hot sauce for drizzling (we used Sriracha)

1 In a small bowl smash up the avocado with a fork, leaving some pieces chunky, then add in the lime juice and season to taste.

2 Next heat the oil in a large non-stick frying pan or two smaller frying pans over a medium heat. Add the spiralized red onion and cook for 2 mins until partially softened then stir in the sweet potato. Season with salt and press the potato into the pan with the back of a wooden spoon. Cook for 10–15 mins, stirring occasionally, until the potato is softened and crisping at the edges.

3 Make space in the pan or pans to fry the eggs. If the pan is very dry add a little more oil. Crack in the eggs and cook for a further 2–3 mins until the whites are just set and the yolks runny then dollop on the smashed avo and drizzle with hot sauce to serve.

PER SERVING 558 kcals, fat 32g, sat fat 7g, carbs 47g, sugars 21g, fibre 12g, protein 14g, salt 0.6g

Pastry-less pork pie

Replace pastry with courgettes in this show-stopping picnic pie.

🕐 TAKES hours 10 mins   🕐 SERVES 6–8

- 4–5 large courgettes, cut lengthways into thin slices (use a mandolin if you have one), seedy core reserved and finely chopped
- 1 tbsp olive or rapeseed oil, plus a drizzle
- 50g dried breadcrumbs, plus 2 tbsp
- 1 red onion, finely chopped
- 2 garlic cloves, crushed
- 290g jar red peppers, drained and chopped
- small bunch of parsley, chopped
- zest of 1 lemon
- 1 large egg
- 500g minced pork
- 2 tsp chilli flakes and fennel seeds

1 Heat a griddle pan. Toss the courgette slices in a little oil, then cook in batches until soft and marked with griddle lines. Grease an 18cm springform tin with a little oil and put a circle of baking parchment at the base. Line the tin with the courgettes, overlapping them across the base, up the sides and over the edge, leaving enough overhang to seal the pie. Scatter 2 tbsp breadcrumbs over the base.

2 Heat the oil in a large frying pan, add the onion and cook for 5 mins. Add the courgette core and garlic, cook for 5 mins and set aside.

3 Heat oven to 180C/160C fan/gas 4. Mix the cooled veg with the remaining ingredients and seasoning in a bowl. Pack the mixture into the courgette-lined tin, pressing in firmly and flattening the top. Fold over the overhanging courgettes to cover the top of the pie.

4 Place the tin on a baking tray. Bake for 1 hr 15 mins, then cool in the tin for 10 mins. Remove the pie and pour away any juices. Flip the pie onto a plate so that the neater side faces up. Remove the baking parchment and cool completely before serving.

PER SERVING (8) 178 kcals, fat 9g, sat fat 3g, carbs 8g, sugars 2g, fibre 1g, protein 16g, salt 0.2g

Beef, broccoli and oyster sauce stir-fry

Get the most out of your broccoli and spiralize the stalks to go into your beef stir-fry.

⏱ TAKES 30 mins 🕐 SERVES 4

- 1 tbsp soy sauce
- 1 tbsp Shaoxing (Chinese) rice wine or dry sherry
- 1 tsp sesame oil
- 2 tsp cornflour
- 400g lean steak, cut into thin slices against the grain
- 2 tbsp sunflower or groundnut oil
- 1 red and 1 green pepper, deseeded and cut into chunks
- 1 large broccoli (about 350g), head broken into small florets and stalk trimmed then spiralized into thin noodles
- 2 large carrots (about 240g), ends trimmed and spiralized into thin noodles
- 4 tbsp oyster sauce
- 2 spring onions, thinly sliced on a diagonal

1 In a large bowl mix together the soy sauce, rice wine or sherry, sesame oil and cornflour. Add the sliced steak, mix well so that it is evenly coated then leave to marinate for 20 mins while you prepare the veg.

2 Heat a wok or large frying pan over a high heat. Once roaring hot add in half the oil followed by the marinated beef and stir-fry for 3 mins until brown and crisp. Transfer the meat with a slotted spoon to a plate then carefully wipe clean the pan.

3 Add the remaining oil, peppers and broccoli florets. Stir-fry for a few mins before adding the spiralized carrot and broccoli stalk. Cook for a further minute then stir in the oyster sauce and 50ml water. Bring the sauce up to a simmer then briefly return the beef, along with its juices, to the pan to heat through. Serve immediately topped with the sliced spring onion.

PER SERVING 296 kcals, fat 13g, sat fat 4g, carbs 15g, sugars 9g, fibre 8g, protein 26g, salt 2.3g

Chickpea & coriander burgers

High in fibre and low in fat, these veggie burgers are easy to make and taste delicious.

🕐 TAKES 25 mins   🥡 SERVES 4

- 400g can chickpeas, drained
- zest of 1 lemon, plus juice of ½
- 1 tsp ground cumin
- small bunch of coriander, chopped
- 1 egg
- 100g fresh breadcrumbs
- 1 medium red onion, ½ diced, ½ sliced
- 1 tbsp olive oil
- 4 small wholemeal buns
- 1 large tomato, sliced,
- ½ cucumber, sliced
- chilli sauce, to serve

1 In a food processor, whizz the chickpeas, lemon zest and juice, cumin, half the coriander, the egg and some seasoning. Scrape into a bowl and mix with 80g of the breadcrumbs and the diced onions. Form 4 burgers, press remaining breadcrumbs onto both sides and chill on a baking tray for at least 10 mins.

2 Heat the oil in a frying pan until hot. Fry the burgers for 4 mins each side, keeping the heat on medium so they don't burn.

3 To serve, slice each bun and fill with a slice of tomato, a burger, a few red onion slices, some cucumber slices, a dollop of chilli sauce and the remaining coriander.

PER SERVING 344 kcals, fat 8g, sat fat 1g, carbs 56g, sugars 6g, fibre 6g, protein 15g, salt 1.3g

Roasted cauliflower tabbouleh

Replace the grains in this tabbouleh with whizzed-up cauliflower roasted with cinnamon and allspice.

🕐 TAKES 25 mins   🥧 SERVES 4

- 1 large cauliflower, core removed and florets roughly chopped
- 1 tsp ground cinnamon and allspice
- 2 tbsp olive oil
- 25g flaked almonds, toasted
- 1 red onion, finely chopped
- 200g pack feta, crumbled
- 110g tub pomegranate seeds
- juice of 1 lemon
- ½ small pack of parsley, finely chopped
- ½ small pack of mint, finely chopped, plus a few leaves reserved

1 Heat oven to 200C/180C fan/gas 6. Put the cauliflower in the large bowl of a food processor, blitz for 30 secs until it resembles couscous grains, then tip into a large bowl.

2 Mix the spices and olive oil into the cauliflower and season to taste. Spread the cauliflower 'couscous' out on a large baking tray in an even, thin layer. Roast for 12 mins, mixing halfway through so that it is evenly toasted, then set aside to cool slightly.

3 Once at room temperature, stir through the remaining ingredients and season to taste, then sprinkle over the mint leaves.

PER SERVING 319 kcals, fat 21g, sat fat 8g, carbs 14g, sugars 11g, fibre 5g, protein 16g, salt 1.9g

Kale power salad

Packed full of vitamins, this tasty gluten-free and vegan salad with caramelised tamari pumpkin seeds contains all of your five-a-day.

🕐 TAKES 35 mins 🕑 SERVES 2

- 1 large sweet potato (200g), peeled, ends trimmed and spiralized into thin noodles, any very long strands cut into short lengths
- 400g can chickpeas, drained and rinsed
- 2 tbsp extra virgin olive oil, plus extra for drizzling
- 1 tsp smoked paprika
- 100g kale, stalks removed and leaves shredded
- juice of 1 lemon
- 2 tbsp pumpkin seeds
- 2 tsp tamari
- 1 ripe avocado, sliced
- 1 red pepper, deseeded and chopped into small cubes
- 1 small red onion, ends trimmed and spiralized into thin noodles, then cut into shorter lengths

1 Heat oven to 200C/180 fan/gas 6. Keeping the two separate, spread the sweet potato and chickpeas out onto a large baking tray. Drizzle with 1 tbsp of the oil, smoked paprika and season with salt and pepper. Roast for 15–20 mins until the sweet potato is softened and caramelizing at the edges and the chickpeas are golden brown. The potato may cook quicker than the chickpeas so keep an eye on them.

2 In a large bowl massage the kale with the remaining oil, half the lemon juice and some flaky sea salt, then leave to tenderize.

3 Toast the pumpkin seeds in a dry frying pan on a low heat for 2 mins until they start to pop then pour in the tamari. Immediately tip the seeds onto a piece of baking parchment. Once cool, break into pieces.

4 Cover the cut avocado with the remaining lemon juice to stop it browning. Arrange all the components next to each other in a bowl. Drizzle with oil and top with the pumpkin seeds and some seasoning.

PER SERVING 677 kcals, fat 36g, sat fat 6g, carbs 59g, sugars 20g, fibre 18g, protein 19g, salt 0.9g

Thai beef salad

Seared rump steak and chilli dressing add punch to this spiralized salad.

🕐 TAKES 35 mins   📑 SERVES 2

- 1 cucumber, ends trimmed, halved widthways and spiralized into thin noodles then patted dry
- 1 mooli, ends trimmed, halved widthways and spiralized into thin noodles, any very long strands cut in half
- 2 tsp groundnut or sunflower oil
- 1 rump steak (200-250g)
- 100g beansprouts
- 1 small pack of coriander, leaves picked

FOR THE DRESSING
- 1 garlic clove, crushed
- 1 tbsp fish sauce
- 1 tbsp palm or soft brown sugar
- zest and juice of ½ lime
- 1 red chilli, finely chopped and deseeded, if you like

1 Mix all the dressing ingredients together in a small bowl, stirring until the sugar has dissolved. In a large bowl toss the spiralized cucumber and mooli with half of the dressing.

2 Season the steak on both sides and heat the oil in a frying pan until it is searing. Fry the steak for 2–3 mins on each side for medium rare, transfer to a plate to rest for 5 mins, then thinly slice.

3 To assemble the salad, pile the veg onto plates and mix with the beansprouts and coriander. Top with the thinly sliced steak and remaining dressing.

PER SERVING 351 kcals, fat 16g, sat fat 5g, carbs 18g, sugars 16g, fibre 3g, protein 32g, salt 1.8g

Beetroot, halloumi, orange & watercress salad

Griddled halloumi and roasted beetroot are given a Spanish twist with orange, almonds and sherry vinegar.

🕑 TAKES 40 mins   🍳 SERVES 4

- 4 large raw beetroot (about 500g), peeled, ends trimmed and spiralized into thin noodles, any very long strands cut in half
- 3 tbsp extra virgin olive oil
- 1 tbsp sherry vinegar
- 3 oranges (about 840g), peeled and segmented, the juice squeezed from the pith and reserved
- 100g watercress
- 250g pack of halloumi, cut into 4 slices
- 50g almonds, toasted and roughly chopped

1 Heat oven to 200C/180C fan/gas 6. Toss the spiralized beetroot with 1 tbsp of the oil and some seasoning on a large baking tray. Spread out so that the beetroot cooks evenly then roast for 15 mins until tender.

2 Meanwhile, make the dressing by mixing the remaining oil, sherry vinegar and orange juice together in a large bowl. Add the orange juice in increments, adjusting to taste.

3 Toss the watercress and cooked beetroot in half the dressing. Pepper the halloumi on both sides and heat a griddle pan over a high heat. Fry the cheese for 1–2 mins on each side until visibly charred.

4 Divide the beetroot and watercress between plates, scatter over the orange segments and almonds then top with a piece of halloumi. Serve the remaining dressing on the side.

PER SERVING 494 kcals, fat 31g, sat fat 12g, carbs 29g, sugars 28g, fibre 6g, protein 22g, salt 2.1g

Hot-smoked salmon salad

Using frozen peas and broad beans in this salad is a cost-effective way of getting more veg into your diet.

🕐 TAKES 25 mins 📖 SERVES 4

- 200g frozen peas
- 300g frozen podded broad beans
- 1 large cucumber, ends trimmed, halved widthways and spiralized into thick ribbons then patted dry, any very long strands cut in half
- 150g pack of mixed radishes, cut into different shapes
- 4 spring onions, thinly sliced on a diagonal
- 180g hot-smoked salmon fillets, flaked
- 50g pea shoots

FOR THE DRESSING
- juice of 1 lemon
- 1 tsp wholegrain mustard and honey
- 3 tbsp extra virgin olive oil

1 Bring a pan of salted water to the boil. Tip in the peas, cook for 2 mins then remove with a slotted spoon and immediately plunge into a bowl of ice-cold water. Once cold, drain, and transfer the peas to a large salad bowl or sharing platter.

2 Repeat with the broad beans. Once cool, pop the beans from their tough outer skins then mix with the peas.

3 Combine the dressing ingredients together in a small bowl with some seasoning. Mix together all of the remaining components with the peas and beans then toss through the dressing to serve, keeping some on the side.

PER SERVING 300 kcals, fat 14g, sat fat 2g, carbs 17g, sugars 7g, fibre 11g, protein 22g, salt 1.5g

Courgetti, peach, mozzarella & basil salad

Grilled peaches become smoky and carmelized. They are perfectly paired with fresh courgette and creamy mozzarella.

🕐 TAKES 15 mins   🥄 SERVES 2

- 1 large courgette (about 150g), ends trimmed and spiralized into thin noodles, any very long strands cut in half
- 1½ tbsp extra virgin olive oil plus extra for drizzling
- juice of ½ lemon
- 2 ripe but firm peaches, stone removed and each cut into 6 wedges
- 125g ball of buffalo mozzarella, torn
- ½ small pack of basil, leaves picked

1 In a large bowl toss the spiralized courgette with 1 tbsp oil, lemon juice and some flaky sea salt.

2 Heat a griddle pan until searing. Brush the peaches lightly with the remaining oil and griddle for 1–2 mins on each side. You want the peaches to have char marks and become slightly caramelized.

3 Divide the courgetti between plates, scatter over the grilled peaches, mozzarella and basil leaves then finish with a good grinding of pepper and a drizzle of oil.

PER SERVING 309 kcals, fat 21g, sat fat 10g, carbs 13g, sugars 12g, fibre 4g, protein 14g, salt 0.6g

Chicken, pomegranate & carrot salad

Harissa yoghurt adds a kick to this vibrant chicken salad.

TAKES 35 mins   SERVES 4

- 7 large carrots (about 800g), ends trimmed and spiralized into thin noodles, any very long strands cut in half
- 2 tbsp extra virgin olive oil
- zest and juice of 1 lemon
- 400g cooked chicken, torn into pieces
- 1 small pack of mint, leaves picked and roughly chopped, smaller leaves left whole
- 30g pine nuts, toasted
- 100g pomegranate seeds
- 150g pot natural yoghurt
- 1–2 tbsp harissa (depending on how spicy you like it)

1 In a large bowl toss the spiralized carrot with the olive oil, lemon zest, half the lemon juice, some flaky sea salt and black pepper. Leave to marinate for 30 mins if you have time.

2 Toss through the chicken, mint, pine nuts and pomegranate seeds, mixing well with your hands to combine. Divide the salad among plates or pile onto a large platter.

3 In a small bowl mix the yoghurt with the remaining lemon juice, then swirl through the harissa. Serve the yoghurt with the salad.

PER SERVING 426 kcals, fat 21g, sat fat 4g, carbs 22g, sugars 21g, fibre 9g, protein 32g, salt 0.5g

Prawn, avocado & cucumber salad

Cashews, chilli, sesame and soy dressing give the classic prawn and avocado salad a makeover.

🕐 TAKES 15 mins 🫗 SERVES 4

- 300g cooked, peeled king prawns, patted dry
- 120g baby spinach, washed and dried
- 2 avocados, sliced
- 1 large cucumber, ends trimmed, halved widthways and spiralized into thick ribbons then patted dry, any very long strands cut in half
- 50g cashew nuts, toasted and roughly chopped

FOR THE DRESSING
- 1 red chilli, finely chopped and deseeded, if you like
- zest and juice of 1 lime
- 1½ tbsp sesame oil
- 1½ tbsp soy sauce

1 Mix all the dressing ingredients together in a large bowl with some black pepper. Tip in the prawns and leave to marinate while you prepare the rest of the salad.

2 To assemble, lift the prawns out of the marinade and transfer to a plate then toss the spinach in the remaining dressing. Add in the avocado and cucumber and carefully toss to combine.

3 Divide the salad between plates, top with the prawns and chopped cashews.

Asian chicken salad

· ·

This easy-to-prepare salad with separate salad dressing makes a tasty, take-to-work lunch.

🕐 TAKES 15 mins   🍳 SERVES 2

- ½ cucumber, end trimmed and spiralized into thin noodles
- 2 carrots, ends trimmed and spiralized into thin noodles
- 100g bag crisp salad leaves (a mix of radicchio, frisée and round lettuce)
- 4 spring onions, thinly sliced
- 200g pack roast chicken pieces
- 2 tsp sesame seeds

FOR THE DRESSING
- 2 tbsp sesame oil
- 1½ tbsp rice wine vinegar
- 1½ tbsp low-salt soy sauce
- ½ tbsp freshly grated ginger
- 1 tsp golden caster sugar

1 Layer the salad ingredients into two plastic containers if you're packing to take to work, or put them in a large bowl.

2 Make the dressing by combining all the ingredients in a jar with a lid, add some seasoning and shake well. Put the dressing in two small pots to pack into your lunchboxes, or toss through the salad if eating it straight away.

· ·

PER SERVING 277 kcals, fat 8g, sat fat 1g, carbs 14g, sugars 13g, fibre 5g, protein 35g, salt 1.6g

Broccoli, green bean and flaked almond salad

Roasting broccoli brings out its nutty flavour, which is enhanced in this salad by toasted almonds and tahini yoghurt.

🕐 TAKES 30 mins   👐 SERVES 2

- 1 broccoli head, head cut into florets, stalk spiralized
- 2 tbsp olive oil
- 1 tsp sumac
- 120g pack green beans
- 1 tbsp toasted flaked almonds
- ½ small pack of parsley, roughly chopped

FOR THE YOGHURT DRESSING
- 150g pot of natural yoghurt
- juice of ½ lemon
- 2 tbsp tahini paste

1 Heat oven to 200C/180C fan/gas 6. Put the florets onto a baking tray, drizzle over the oil and sumac then season with sea salt and black pepper. Roast for 20 mins, turning halfway until the florets are slightly charred and completely tender.

2 Meanwhile mix all the ingredients together with some seasoning in a small bowl for the yoghurt dressing, letting it down with a splash of water so that it is a drizzling consistency.

3 Once the roasted broccoli is nearly cooked bring a small pan of salted water to the boil. Plunge in the green beans and cook for 1½ mins, then add the spiralized broccoli stalk. Cook for a further 30 seconds then drain.

4 Toss all the veg together on two plates or a platter, drizzle over the yoghurt dressing then scatter over the toasted flaked almonds and parsley to serve.

PER SERVING 341 kcals, fat 24g, sat fat 4g, carbs 11g, sugars 8g, fibre 11g, protein 15g, salt 0.3g

Waldorf salad

· ·

Spiralized apple, chicory and tarragon lend a modern twist to this classic salad.

🕐 TAKES 25 mins 🕐 SERVES 2

- 2 Cox apples, spiralized into thin noodles, any very long strands cut in half
- juice ½ lemon
- 2 celery sticks, thinly sliced
- 30g walnuts, toasted and roughly chopped
- 10 mixed grapes, (about 75g) halved
- 140g red chicory, leaves torn

FOR THE DRESSING
- 100ml natural yoghurt
- juice of ½ lemon
- handful of tarragon leaves, finely chopped

1 Combine the yoghurt, lemon and tarragon together in a large bowl with some flaky sea salt and black pepper.
2 Mix the apple with the lemon juice to stop it turning brown then toss together with the remaining salad ingredients in a large bowl then divide between plates and drizzle over the yoghurt dressing.

· ·
PER SERVING 225 kcals, fat 13g, sat fat 2g, carbs 19g, sugars 18g, fibre 3g, protein 7g, salt 0.2g

Chicken, broccoli & beetroot salad with avocado pesto

Swap the chicken for tofu for a delicious vegan alternative.

🕐 TAKES 30 mins   📖 SERVES 4

- 250g tenderstem broccoli
- 2 tsp rapeseed oil
- 3 skinless chicken breasts
- 1 red onion, thinly sliced
- 100g bag watercress
- 2 raw beetroots (about 175g), peeled and grated
- 1 tsp nigella seeds

FOR THE AVOCADO PESTO

- 1 avocado, peeled and stone removed
- small pack basil, leaves picked
- ½ garlic clove, crushed
- 25g walnut halves
- 1 tbsp rapeseed oil
- juice and zest of 1 lemon

1 Bring a large pan of water to the boil, add the broccoli and cook for 2 mins. Drain, then refresh under cold water. Heat a griddle pan, toss the broccoli in ½ tsp of the rapeseed oil and griddle for 2–3 mins, turning, until a little charred. Set aside to cool. Brush the chicken with the remaining oil and season. Griddle for 3–4 mins each side or until cooked through. Leave to cool, then slice into chunky pieces.

2 Next, make the pesto. Blitz the avocado, basil, garlic, walnuts and oil with 1 tbsp lemon juice, 2–3 tbsp cold water and some seasoning. Transfer to a small serving dish. Pour the remaining lemon juice over the sliced onions and leave for a few mins.

3 Pile the watercress onto a large platter. Toss through the broccoli and onion, along with the lemon juice they were soaked in. Top with the beetroot, but don't mix it in, and the chicken. Scatter over the reserved basil leaves, the lemon zest and nigella seeds, then serve with the avocado pesto.

PER SERVING 320 kcals, fat 18g, sat fat 3g, carbs 8g, sugars 6g, fibre 6g, protein 29g, salt 0.3g

Herby courgette & quinoa salad

Fresh herbs add bags of flavour to this quinoa salad - we used mint and parsley but play around with your favourite.

🕐 TAKES 25 mins   🄯 SERVES 3

- 150g quinoa
- 2 courgettes (about 375g), ends trimmed, halved widthways and spiralized into thin noodles, any very long strands cut in half
- 1 tsp chilli flakes
- 2 tsp za'atar
- juice of 1 lemon
- 2 tbsp extra virgin olive oil
- 200g cherry tomatoes on the vine, halved
- 1 small pack of mint, chopped
- 1 small pack of parsley, chopped
- 3 tbsp mixed seeds, toasted

1 Rinse the quinoa then put into a saucepan, cover with 300ml cold water and a pinch of sea salt. Bring to the boil then simmer for 15 mins until the grains have doubled in size but still retain their bite.

2 Put the courgettes in a large bowl along with the spices, lemon juice, olive oil, some sea salt and black pepper. Mix well and leave the flavours to infuse.

3 Drain the quinoa then spread out onto a baking tray so that it cools quicker. Once cool stir into the courgettes along with the tomatoes, herbs and mixed seeds. Taste for seasoning then spoon into bowls.

Spiced carrot & spelt salad

This sharing-style salad can be made ahead and looks fantastic, perfect for feeding a crowd.

🕐 TAKES 35 mins   📊 SERVES 6

- 6–7 large carrots (about 700g), ends trimmed and spiralized into thin noodles, any very long strands cut in half
- 2 tbsp olive oil
- 2 tsp ground cumin and coriander
- 2 x 250g pouches of ready cooked spelt
- 1 large pack of parsley, chopped
- 1 large red onion, finely chopped
- 100g sultanas

FOR THE DRESSING
- zest and juice of 1 orange
- 1 tsp honey
- 2 tbsp red wine vinegar
- 3 tbsp extra virgin olive oil

1 Heat oven to 200C/180C fan/gas 6. Toss the spiralized carrot with the oil, spices and some seasoning in a large bowl then divide between two baking trays and roast for 15 mins.

2 Meanwhile, combine the dressing ingredients together in a small bowl and season to taste. After 15 mins, tip the ready cooked spelt over the spiralized carrots and return to the oven for 5 mins to heat through.

3 Once warm, transfer the carrot and spelt to a large salad bowl or sharing platter. Use a spatula to get all the spiced oil off the tray into the salad.

4 Mix through the dressing and all of the other ingredients. Eat warm or make ahead and serve at room temperature.

Greek salad

· ·

Spiralized courgette gives body and freshness to this Greek salad.

🕐 TAKES 15 mins   🍽 SERVES 2

- 1½ tbsp extra virgin olive oil
- juice of ½ lemon
- 2 courgettes, ends trimmed and spiralized into thin noodles
- ½ cucumber, sliced on a diagonal
- 60g feta, crumbled
- 100g green olives
- 100g sundried tomatoes

1 In a large bowl mix together the oil and the lemon juice with some flaky sea salt and black pepper. Add the courgetti and stir well so that every strand is coated in the dressing. Leave to marinate for 5 mins then stir through all the remaining ingredients. Divide between plates to serve.

· ·

PER SERVING 393 kcals, fat 22g, sat fat 6g, carbs 27g, sugars 23g, fibre 10g, protein 16g, salt 2g

Tuna & butterbean salad

Tinned tuna and butterbeans are an economic way of getting fibre and protein into this salad.

🕐 TAKES 20 mins 📖 SERVES 2 generously

- 400g can butterbeans, drained and rinsed
- 1 large courgette, ends trimmed and spiralized into thin noodles, any very long strands cut in half
- 1 small red onion, ends trimmed and spiralized into flat noodles
- 50g black olives, stoned and halved
- 200g cherry tomatoes on the vine, halved
- ½ small pack of parsley, roughly chopped
- 200g can tuna in spring water, drained

FOR THE DRESSING
- 3 tbsp extra virgin olive oil
- 1 tbsp white wine vinegar
- ½ tsp Dijon mustard

1 Whisk the dressing ingredients together in a small bowl with some sea salt and black pepper.

2 Toss all the salad ingredients together, bar the tuna, in a large bowl. Pour over the dressing then flake in the tuna and gently stir to combine. Taste for seasoning then divide between plates.

PER SERVING 432 kcals, fat 23g, sat fat 4g, carbs 23g, sugars 8g, fibre 10g, protein 28g, salt 1.3g

Prosciutto, pear & blue cheese salad

The classic, winning combination of pear, ham and blue cheese is updated using the spiralizer.

🕐 TAKES 15 mins   🥧 SERVES 4

- 3–4 firm but ripe pears (about 500g), pointy end trimmed and spiralized into thin noodles
- juice of 1 lemon
- 2 tbsp extra virgin olive oil
- 1 tbsp balsamic vinegar
- 180g rocket leaves
- 100g creamy blue cheese, crumbled
- 80g pack of prosciutto, torn

1 Mix the spiralized pears in a bowl with the lemon juice to stop them discolouring.
2 In another large bowl mix the olive oil with the balsamic and some seasoning. Tip in the rocket leaves and mix well so that all the leaves get coated in the dressing.
3 Divide the rocket among plates, then scatter over the spiralized pear, blue cheese and ham and a generous grind of black pepper.

PER SERVING 249 kcals, fat 16g, sat fat 7g, carbs 13g, sugars 13g, fibre 4g, protein 12g, salt 1.8g

Som tum salad

This Thai salad packs a punch. If you can't get hold of papaya substitute for firm, under-ripe mango instead.

🕐 TAKES 30 mins   🥧 SERVES 4

- 2 garlic cloves
- 50g roasted peanuts
- 1 tbsp of dried shrimp, rinsed (optional)
- 2 birds eye chillies, sliced
- 200g fine green beans, cut into quarters
- 120g baby plum tomatoes, halved
- 2 tbsp fish sauce
- juice of 1 lime, plus 1 lime cut into 4 wedges
- 2 tbsp palm or soft brown sugar
- 1 green papaya (about 900g), peeled and ends trimmed
- handful of Thai basil, leaves picked

1 Using a pestle and mortar, pound the garlic, pinch of sea salt, half of the peanuts and shrimp (if using) to a rough paste. Add the chilli, green beans and tomatoes and lightly bruise. Transfer everything to a large bowl.

2 Use the pestle and mortar again to mix together the fish sauce, lime juice and sugar, stirring until the sugar has dissolved. Pour the dressing into the bowl with the tomatoes.

3 Spiralize the papaya, starting at one end until you reach the seeds in the middle. Scrape out the seeds, then turn the papaya around and spiralize from the other end until you reach the seeds in the middle again. Add the papaya to the bowl and toss everything together until well coated. Taste for seasoning; you want a good balance of spice, sour, sweet and saltiness, so adjust if necessary.

4 Divide the salad among plates and scatter over the Thai basil and remaining peanuts. Serve with the lime wedges.

PER SERVING 250 kcals, fat 7g, sat fat 1g, carbs 35g, sugars 32g, fibre 10g, protein 7g, salt 1.8g

Summer courgette, kale & goat's cheese salad

Turn leftover bread into crispy croutons in this wholesome summer salad.

🕐 TAKES 25 mins   📖 SERVES 4

- 25g pine nuts
- 4 large courgettes, ends trimmed and spiralized into ribbons
- juice and zest of ½ lemon (save the other ½ for the dressing)
- 1 small loaf of sourdough bread or stale bread
- 1 tbsp olive oil
- 60g bag baby kale
- 100g goat's cheese
- crumbled handful of mint leaves
- picked 25g raisins

FOR THE DRESSING

- 2 tbsp extra virgin olive oil
- 1 tbsp lemon juice
- 1 tbsp clear honey

1 Heat oven to 200C/180C fan/gas 6 and tip the pine nuts onto a baking tray. Put the courgette ribbons in a large bowl with the juice and zest of ½ the lemon. Cut the sourdough into chunky dice and pop on the baking tray, next to the nuts. Drizzle with the oil and add plenty of seasoning.

2 Roast for about 5 mins until the pine nuts are golden and toasted, then remove from the baking tray and set aside. Return the croutons to the oven for a further 5–8 mins until golden.

3 Meanwhile, wash and dry the kale and add to the courgettes with the goat's cheese, mint and raisins. Mix everything together. Make the dressing by combining all the ingredients in a small bowl with some seasoning. Toss through the salad.

4 Pile the salad onto a platter and scatter over the croutons, pine nuts and plenty of black pepper.

PER SERVING 555 kcals, fat 22g, sat fat 7g, carbs 66g, sugars 13g, fibre 4g, protein 21g, salt 1.7g

Goat's cheese, pear & candied pecan salad

Spiralizing the pear and grilling the goat's cheese make this an impressive-looking salad: ideally served as a starter when eating with friends.

TAKES 30 mins   SERVES 4

- 100g pecans
- 2 tbsp soft brown sugar
- 1 tbsp maple syrup
- 2 red-skinned pears, ends trimmed and spiralized into thin noodles
- 100g wild rocket
- 4 x 35g rounds of goat's cheese

FOR THE DRESSING
- 1 tsp mustard powder
- 2 tbsp white wine vinegar
- 4 tbsp extra virgin olive oil

1 Heat oven to 200C/180C fan/gas 6 and put the pecans on a non-stick baking sheet. Sprinkle over the sugar and maple syrup, and toss to combine. Roast for 5–7 mins until caramelised, then leave to cool completely before roughly chopping.

2 Meanwhile, make the dressing by combining the ingredients and seasoning well. In a large bowl, toss the pear with the rocket and with a little of the dressing.

3 Just before serving, blowtorch or grill the goat's cheese rounds until golden. To serve, put the remaining dressing in a squeezy bottle and swirl around the edge of the plate. Put the pear and rocket salad in the middle, scatter over the nuts and top with the goat's cheese.

PER SERVING 487 kcals, fat 38g, sat fat 9g, carbs 22g, sugars 21g, fibre 5g, protein 11g, salt 0.6g

Quinoa stew with squash, prunes & pomegranate

Roasted squash and pomegranate seeds add vibrancy to this quinoa stew.

🕐 TAKES 55 mins   🍽 SERVES 4

- 1 small butternut squash, deseeded and cubed
- 2 tbsp olive oil
- 1 large onion, thinly sliced
- 1 garlic clove, chopped
- 1 tbsp finely chopped ginger
- 1 tsp ras el hanout or Middle Eastern spice mix
- 200g quinoa
- 5 prunes, roughly chopped
- juice of 1 lemon
- 600ml vegetable stock (we used bouillon)
- seeds from 1 pomegranate
- small handful of mint leaves

1 Heat oven to 200C/180C fan/gas 6. Put the squash on a baking tray and toss with 1 tbsp of the oil. Season well and roast for 30–35 mins or until soft.

2 Meanwhile, heat the remaining oil in a big saucepan. Add the onion, garlic and ginger, season and cook for 10 mins. Add the spice and quinoa, and cook for another couple of mins. Add the prunes, lemon juice and stock, bring to the boil, then cover and simmer for 25 mins.

3 When everything is tender, stir the squash through the stew. Spoon into bowls and scatter with pomegranate seeds and mint to serve.

PER SERVING 318 kcals, fat 9g, sat fat 1g, carbs 50g, sugars 20g, fibre 6g, protein 11g, salt 0.5g

Hearty pistou soup

Get all of your five-a-day in this gutsy root vegetable soup with basil pistou, a French take on classic pesto.

TAKES 45 mins   SERVES 6

- 2 tbsp olive oil, plus drizzling
- 2 large leeks (about 300g), and 2 celery sticks, thinly sliced
- 1 large fennel bulb (about 300g), thinly sliced
- 3 large carrots (about 320g), ends trimmed, halved widthways and spiralized into thin noodles
- 1 small celeriac, peeled, ends trimmed, halved and spiralized into thin noodles
- 2 turnips peeled, ends trimmed and spiralized into thin noodles
- 2 x 400g cans haricot beans, drained and rinsed
- 2 bay leaves
- 3 garlic cloves, peeled and finely chopped

FOR THE PISTOU

- 1 large pack of basil, leaves picked and torn
- 2 large garlic cloves, peeled
- 6 tbsp extra virgin olive oil
- 60g Parmesan, finely grated

1 Heat the oil in a large saucepan over a low to medium heat. Add the leek, celery, fennel, carrot, celeriac and turnip. Cook gently for 8 mins until softened but not coloured. Increase the heat slightly and stir in the bay leaves and garlic. Cook for a further min then pour over 1.5 litres of water. Bring to the boil then reduce to a simmer and add the beans. Simmer the soup gently for 5 mins until all the veg are tender but holding their shape.

2 While the soup is simmering away, pound the garlic in a pestle and mortar with a little salt. Add the basil leaves and continue to pound until a rough paste then stir in the oil and Parmesan.

3 Taste the soup for seasoning and adjust to taste, then ladle into bowls and top with a spoonful of the pistou.

PER SERVING 299 kcals, fat 18g, sat fat 3g, carbs 17g, sugars 8g, fibre 16g, protein 10g, salt 0.4g

Green gazpacho

The flavours in this chilled soup will develop as it sits, but if you are a fan of heat, serve with some extra chopped jalapeños.

🕐 TAKES 20 mins plus chilling   🥧 SERVES 2

- 150g pot natural yoghurt
- 2 pickled jalapeños and ½ tbsp of their pickling juice
- ½ small pack of basil
- ½ small pack of mint, plus a few extra leaves reserved to garnish
- 1 small ripe avocado, peeled and covered with the juice of ½ lemon to stop it discolouring
- 50g baby spinach leaves
- 2 spring onions, roughly chopped
- 1 garlic clove, peeled
- 1 large cucumber, ends trimmed then half roughly chopped and half spiralized into ribbons and patted dry
- drizzle of extra virgin olive oil

1 Put all the ingredients except the spiralized cucumber, reserved mint leaves and olive oil into a food processor along with a good pinch of salt and pepper and blitz until smooth. Taste for seasoning, then add enough water to get your desired soup consistency.

2 Chill the soup for at least 2 hours until it is very cold. Serve in chilled bowls topped with the spiralized cucumber, mint leaves and a drizzle of oil.

PER SERVING 207 kcals, fat 14g, sat fat 4g, carbs 10g, sugars 8g, fibre 4g, protein 8g, salt 1.1g

Spicy chicken & chorizo one pot

Sure to become a family favourite, adjust the amount of harissa in this one pot to suit your taste.

🕐 TAKES 1 hr 15 mins 🍽 SERVES 4

- 1 tbsp olive oil
- 4 skinless boneless chicken breasts (500g)
- 100g cooking chorizo, peeled and cut into slices
- 2 red onions, ends trimmed and spiralized into flat noodles, strands cut in half
- 3 garlic cloves, crushed
- 2 large red peppers, deseeded and cut into slices
- 1–2 tbsp harissa paste (depending on your taste)
- 1 tsp smoked paprika
- 2 x 400g can of chopped tomatoes
- 1 bay leaf
- 3 large potatoes (about 500g), peeled, ends trimmed and spiralized into thin noodles
- 1 small pack of parsley, roughly chopped
- green salad, to serve (optional)

1 Heat the oil in a large flameproof casserole dish or heavy-based saute pan over a medium to high heat. Season the chicken breasts, brown on both sides for around 3 mins, then transfer to a plate.

2 Add in the sliced chorizo and cook for 2 mins until the oils have been released then reduce the heat and add the onions. Cook gently for 10 mins until softened then add in the garlic and peppers and cook for a further minute.

3 Turn up the heat and spoon in the harissa and paprika, fry, stirring constantly for 1–2 mins until fragrant then pour in the chopped tomatoes along with one of the tomato cans filled with water. Bring to the boil, reduce to a simmer and add the bay leaf, potatoes, chicken and some seasoning.

4 Cover and leave to simmer away for 20–25 mins, until everything is cooked through, then remove the bay and scatter over the chopped parsley. Serve with a green salad, if you like.

PER SERVING 461 kcals, fat 13g, sat fat 4g, carbs 38g, sugars 17g, fibre 8g, protein 42g, salt 1.2g

Curried parsnip soup

Make extra of the parsnip crisps and store in an airtight container for snacking purposes.

🕐 TAKES 1 hr 5 mins   📋 SERVES 4

- 1 tsp cumin and coriander seeds
- ½ tsp turmeric and ground ginger
- 2 tbsp groundnut or sunflower oil
- 1kg parsnips, 700g peeled and chopped, 300g ends trimmed, spiralized using the straight blade into flat ribbons and then cut into round slices
- 1 large onion, peeled and chopped
- 2 garlic cloves, crushed
- 1 litre low-sodium vegetable stock (we used bouillon)

1 Heat oven to 220C/200C fan/gas 8 and line a large baking sheet with baking parchment. Toast the seeds in a dry frying pan for 1 min until beginning to pop. Grind in a pestle and mortar, then stir in the ground spices.
2 Transfer half of the spice mix to a large bowl along with 1 tbsp oil. Toss in the spiralized parsnip with some seasoning then spread out onto the baking tray. Roast for 20 mins, turning halfway, until completely crisp. Keep checking; some crisps cook faster than others.
3 Meanwhile, heat the remaining oil in a large saucepan over a low heat. Tip in the onion and cook gently for 10 mins then stir in the remaining spice mix and crushed garlic. Cook for 1–2 mins, until fragrant.
4 Add the chopped parsnips, the stock and some seasoning. Bring to the boil then simmer gently for 30 mins until the parsnips are completely tender. Taste for seasoning then blitz until smooth. Ladle the soup into bowls and top with the parsnip crisps.

PER SERVING 144 kcals, fat 6g, sat fat 1g, carbs 16g, sugars 8g, fibre 5g, protein 2g, salt 0.2g

Prawn laksa

· ·

Ready in 15 mins, this Malaysian inspired soup is perfect for when you are time poor but want a bowl of something warm and nourishing quickly.

🕐 TAKES 15 mins   🕒 SERVES 2

- 1 tsp sunflower or groundnut oil
- 1 garlic clove, grated
- small piece of ginger, grated
- 2–3 tbsp Thai green curry paste (depending on how spicy you like it)
- 400ml can coconut milk
- 150g pack cooked tiger prawns
- 2 courgettes, ends trimmed and spiralized into thin noodles

1 Heat the oil in a sauté pan over a medium heat. Add the garlic and ginger, cook out for 1 min until smelling fragrant then stir in the curry paste. Continue to cook for another minute, stirring, then pour in the coconut milk. Bring to the boil then reduce the heat and let the sauce bubble away for a few mins to thicken slightly.

2 Tip in the cooked prawns and courgetti. Cook for 1 min to warm through, then divide between bowls.

· ·

PER SERVING 479 kcals, fat 39g, sat fat 30g, carbs 11g, sugars 7g, fibre 4g, protein 18g, salt 1.8g

Sausage & puy lentil stew

We used pork sausages in this stew but feel free to mix it up with your favourite.

🕐 TAKES 1 hr 25 mins 🕐 SERVES 3

- 1 tbsp olive oil
- 6 good-quality sausages
- 1 large onion, ends trimmed and spiralized into flat noodles, any very long strands cut in half
- 1 large carrot (about 120g), ends trimmed, halved widthways and spiralized into thin noodles
- 1 celery stick, thinly sliced
- 2 garlic cloves, crushed
- 1 bay leaf
- 2 sprigs of rosemary
- 150g puy lentils
- 500ml good-quality chicken stock
- ½ celeriac (about 400g), peeled, ends trimmed, halved and spiralized into thin noodles any very long strands cut in half
- 1 tbsp sherry vinegar

1 Heat the oil in a flameproof casserole dish or heavy-based sauté pan over a medium heat. Add the sausages and cook for 8–10 mins until nicely browned. Transfer to a plate using a slotted spoon.

2 Reduce the heat and stir in the onion, carrot and celery. Cook gently for 10 mins until softened then add the garlic, bay, rosemary and lentils. Cook for 1 min then return the sausages to the pan.

3 Pour over the stock and some seasoning, bring to the boil then reduce and gently simmer for 30 mins before adding the celeriac. If the stew looks a little dry at this point, add some water.

4 Give everything a good stir then cook for a further 15 mins until most of the liquid has been absorbed and the lentils and celeriac are tender. Stir in the sherry vinegar, taste for seasoning, remove the herbs and serve with a green salad.

PER SERVING 653 kcals, fat 33g, sat fat 11g, carbs 45g, sugars 13g, fibre 19g, protein 33g, salt 2.1g

Honey & mustard chicken with chard

Using chicken legs on the bone adds depth of flavour to this creamy dish.

 TAKES 1hr 35 mins SERVES 4

- 1 tbsp olive oil
- 4 chicken legs, skin on and bone in
- 2 onions, ends trimmed and spiralized into flat noodles, any very long strands cut in half
- 4 thyme sprigs
- 1 tbsp clear honey
- 3 tbsp wholegrain mustard
- 300ml low-sodium vegetable stock (we used bouillon)
- 1 large swede (about 850g), peeled, ends trimmed, halved and spiralized into thin noodles any very long strands cut in half
- 500g chard, stalks removed and shredded
- 2 tbsp crème fraiche

1 Heat oven to 180C/160C fan/gas 4. Heat the oil in a large flameproof casserole dish over a medium heat. Season the chicken legs and fry for 10 mins until golden brown then transfer to a plate.

2 Reduce the heat, add the onions and cook gently for 5 mins until partially softened. Return the chicken to the pan and scatter over the thyme. Mix the honey and mustard with the veg stock and some seasoning.

3 Pour over the chicken, bring to the boil then cover and put in the oven to roast for 50 mins then lift the chicken onto a plate, stir in the swede put the chicken back on top and return to the oven for 15 mins until both are very tender.

4 Just before serving put the chard in a large microwaveable bowl with a dash of water. Cover and cook on high for 2 mins, or until wilted. Remove the chicken from the oven and stir in the crème fraiche. If the sauce is a little thin, bubble on the stove for a few mins to reduce.

PER SERVING 477 kcals, fat 29g, sat fat 10g, carbs 18g, sugars 14g, fibre 5g, protein 32g, salt 1.7g

Supergreen soup with yoghurt & pine nuts

A simple, low-fat soup that is a fresh way to use a bag of mixed salad leaves.

🕐 TAKES 30 mins   🕑 SERVES 2

- 2 tsp olive oil
- 1 onion, chopped
- 2 garlic cloves, crushed
- 1 potato (approx 250g), cut into small cubes
- 600ml vegetable stock (we used bouillon)
- 120g bag mixed watercress, rocket and spinach salad
- 150g pot natural yoghurt
- 20g pine nuts, toasted
- chilli oil, to serve (optional)

1 Heat the oil in a medium saucepan over a low-medium heat. Add the onion and a pinch of salt, then cook slowly, stirring occasionally, for 10 mins until softened but not coloured. Add the garlic and cook for 1 min more.

2 Tip in the potato followed by the vegetable stock. Simmer for 10–12 mins until the potato is soft enough that a cutlery knife will slide in easily. Add the bag of salad and let it wilt for 1 min, then blitz the soup in a blender until it's completely smooth.

3 Serve with a drizzle of yoghurt, some toasted pine nuts and some chilli oil, if you like.

1 PER SERVING 325 kcals, fat 13g, sat fat 2g, carbs 36g, sugars 14g, fibre 7g, protein 12g, salt 1g

Beef, miso & spiralized mooli broth with an egg

Boiling the egg for this soup for 6 mins will give you a perfectly runny yolk.

🕐 TAKES 30 mins   👐 SERVES 2

- 600ml low-sodium vegetable stock
- 2 tbsp miso paste
- a small piece of ginger, cut into two slices
- 1 star anise
- 1 (200g) sirloin steak
- ½ tbsp olive oil
- 100g shiitake mushrooms, halved if large
- 2 bulbs of pak choi (about 200g), shredded
- 1 mooli (daikon radish), ends trimmed and spiralized into thin noodles
- 2 large eggs, soft-boiled for 6 mins, rinsed under cold water, peeled and halved
- handful of coriander, leaves picked

1 Bring the stock to a gentle boil in a medium saucepan. Stir in the miso paste, ginger and star anise then leave to simmer over a medium heat while you fry the steak.

2 Season the steak on both sides with salt and pepper then heat the oil in a frying pan until searing hot. Fry the steak for 2 mins on each side for medium rare, then transfer to a plate to rest.

3 Add the mushrooms, pak choi and spiralized mooli to the broth. Simmer for 3–4 mins, until everything is tender. Thinly slice the steak then divide the broth and vegetables between bowls. Top each with half the steak, a soft-boiled egg and some coriander.

PER SERVING 381 kcals, fat 20g, sat fat 7g, carbs 17g, sugars 8g, fibre 2g, protein 33g, salt 2.4g

Beetroot & apple soup

A take on Eastern European borscht, the apple and caraway seeds bring this beetroot soup up to date.

🕐 TAKES 1 hr 10 mins   ⏱ SERVES 4

- 1 tbsp olive oil
- 1 onion, chopped
- 1 carrot, peeled and chopped
- 1 celery stick, peeled and chopped
- 2 fat garlic cloves, crushed
- 1 tsp caraway seeds
- 3 Cox apples, 1 cored and chopped the other 2 trimmed and spiralized into thin noodles just before serving, any very long strands cut in half
- 500g raw beetroot, peeled and cut into small cubes
- 800ml low-sodium vegetable stock
- juice of ½ lemon
- dill and crème fraiche, to serve (optional)

1 Heat the oil in a large saucepan over a low to medium heat. Add the onion, carrot, celery and a pinch of salt then cook gently for 10 mins until softened but not coloured. Next stir in the garlic, caraway seeds, chopped apple and beetroot. Continue to cook gently for 15 mins.

2 Pour over the veg stock, bring to the boil then reduce the heat and simmer gently for 20 mins until the beetroot is completely tender. Taste for seasoning then blitz the soup until it is completely smooth.

3 In a small bowl toss the spiralized apple with the lemon juice to stop it from discolouring. Serve the soup hot or cold topped with the spiralized apple, some dill and crème fraiche, if using.

PER SERVING 143 kcals, fat 4g, sat fat 1g, carbs 21g, sugars 18g, fibre 6g, protein 4g, salt 0.4g

Late summer minestrone

Hold on to the last days of summer with this vibrant tomato, oregano and courgette minestrone.

🕐 TAKES 1 hr   🕐 SERVES 6-8

- 1 tbsp olive oil
- 100g smoked pancetta cubes
- 1 large red onion, ends trimmed and spiralized into flat noodles
- 2 carrots, peeled, halved widthways, ends trimmed and spiralized into thin noodles
- 2 celery sticks, peeled and chopped
- 4 garlic cloves, peeled and finely chopped
- handful of oregano, leaves picked
- 200g Swiss chard, leaves and stalks chopped
- 2 x 400g cans good-quality plum tomatoes
- 500ml chicken stock
- 400g can cannellini beans, drained and rinsed
- 3 courgettes, ends trimmed and spiralized into thin noodles
- Parmesan, to serve

1 Heat 1 tsp of oil in a large saucepan over a medium heat. Add the smoked pancetta and cook for 5 mins, until crisp. Transfer to a plate using a slotted spoon.

2 Pour the remaining oil into the pan, lower the heat and add the spiralized onion, carrot, celery, garlic, oregano and chard stalks. Cook gently, stirring occasionally, for 10 mins until softened but not coloured.

3 Return the pancetta to the pan then tip in the plum tomatoes, chicken stock and cannellini beans. Bring to the boil then simmer gently for 15 mins.

4 Try the soup, seasoning to taste, then stir in the chard leaves and spiralized courgette. Cook for a further 2–3 mins until both are tender then ladle the soups into bowls and serve with Parmesan at the table.

PER SERVING (8) 151 kcals, fat 6g, sat fat 2g, carbs 13g, sugars 8g, fibre 5g, protein 10g, salt 0.7g

Lamb, apricot & pistachio tagine

Replace couscous with spiralized carrot in this fruity and fragrant lamb tagine.

🕐 TAKES 1 hr 50 mins 🥧 SERVES 6-8

- 4 tbsp olive oil
- 1kg lean lamb, diced
- 4 large onions, ends trimmed and spiralized into flat noodles, strands cut in half
- 6 garlic cloves, crushed
- 2–3 tbsp ras el hanout
- 2 tsp hot paprika
- 2 x 400g cans chopped tomatoes
- 200g soft dried apricots, halved
- 700ml chicken stock
- 2 x 400g cans chickpeas, drained and rinsed
- 6 large carrots (about 700g), ends trimmed and spiralized into thin noodles any very long strands cut in half
- 2 preserved lemons, interior pulp discarded and skin finely chopped
- 80g pistachios, toasted and roughly chopped

1 Heat oven to 180C/160C fan/gas 4. Heat half the oil in the largest heavy bottomed, flameproof casserole dish you have, over a medium to high heat. Season the lamb, then working in batches (with the oil as well), brown the meat all over then remove with a slotted spoon and transfer to a plate.

2 Tip in the onions and cook for 2–3 mins until golden then add the garlic and cook for 1 min more. Stir in the dried spices, mix everything together and cook for a further min until fragrant. Return the lamb to the pan then tip in the chopped tomatoes, apricots and some seasoning. Pour in the stock then cover and cook in the oven for 1 hour and 15 mins. Check occasionally to make sure there is enough liquid in the casserole and top up if you need to.

3 After this time add the chickpeas, carrot and preserved lemon to the tagine and return to the oven for 15 mins until the lamb is tender. Scatter over the pistachios and serve.

PER SERVING 586 kcals, fat 27g, sat fat 8g, carbs 42g, sugars 27g, fibre 15g, protein 38g, salt 0.6g

Kale, chickpea & butternut squash stew

Warm up with this hearty, spiced coconut vegan stew.

🕐 TAKES 45 mins   📋 SERVES 3-4

- 1 tbsp coconut oil
- 1 onion, ends trimmed and spiralized into flat noodles, any very long strands cut in half
- 1 garlic clove, finely chopped
- 1 red chilli, finely chopped and deseeded if you like
- ½ tsp turmeric, ground cumin and ground coriander
- 400ml can coconut milk
- 500ml low-sodium vegetable stock
- 400g can chickpeas, drained and rinsed
- 1 medium butternut squash (about 850g), peeled, ends trimmed, cut in half widthways and spiralized into thin noodles, any very long strands cut in half
- 200g shredded kale
- warmed chapatti, to serve (optional)

1 Heat the oil over a low to medium heat in a sauté pan. Add the onion and cook gently for 10 mins to soften without colouring. Stir in the garlic and chilli and cook for 1 min then add the dry spices. Give everything a good mix so that the onion is well coated. Cook out for a further min until fragrant.

2 Pour in the coconut milk, stock and some seasoning. Bring to the boil then reduce to a simmer and add the chickpeas and spiralized butternut. Cook for 6–8 mins until the noodles are nearly tender then stir in the shredded kale.

3 Once the kale has wilted, approx. 2 mins, taste for seasoning then serve the stew with warmed chapatti, if you like.

PER SERVING (4) 404 kcals, fat 22g, sat fat 17g, carbs 35g, sugars 12g, fibre 9g, protein 10g, salt 0.2g

Spring lemon chicken stew

Make the most of the British asparagus season (from the end of April to the end of June) in this fresh lemony dish.

 TAKES 1 hr 10 mins SERVES 2

- 1 tbsp olive oil
- 4 skin-on, boneless chicken thighs
- 1 fat garlic clove, finely chopped
- 150ml white wine
- 400ml good-quality chicken stock
- handful of oregano, leaves picked and roughly chopped
- zest and juice of ½ lemon
- 100g peas (frozen is fine)
- 100g asparagus tips, cut into quarters
- 1 large courgette, ends trimmed and spiralized into thin noodles

1 Heat the oil in a casserole dish or sauté pan over a medium to high heat. Season the chicken thighs then fry until golden brown on both sides, about 10 mins.

2 Drain away any excess fat from the pan then stir in the garlic and cook for a further min then add the white wine. Let it reduce by half then pour in the chicken stock, oregano, lemon zest, juice and some seasoning. Bring to the boil then reduce the heat to a simmer and leave to gently bubble away for 35 mins, until the chicken is cooked through but still juicy.

3 Add the peas, asparagus and spiralized courgette to the pan and simmer for a further 3–4 mins until the veg is tender. If the sauce is a little thin, bubble on the stove for a few mins to reduce.

PER SERVING 564 kcals, fat 31g, sat fat 8g, carbs 11g, sugars 8g, fibre 6g, protein 45g, salt 0.8g

Sweet potato, chilli & lime soup

Warm and comforting, this soup freezes well, so even if dining solo make the full quanity and save the rest.

🕐 TAKES 55 mins 🕐 SERVES 6

- 2½ tbsp. coconut oil
- 2 onions, chopped
- 1.8kg sweet potatoes, 1kg, peeled and chopped into even chunks, 800g peeled, ends trimmed and spiralized into thin noodles
- 2 tsp chilli flakes
- 1.5 litres of low-sodium vegetable stock (we used bouillon)
- zest and juice of 2 limes
- sour cream or coconut yoghurt, to serve

1 Heat oven to 200C/180C fan/gas 6. Heat 2 tbsp of the oil in the largest saucepan you have, over a low to medium heat. Add the onions, cook for 10 mins until softened but not coloured, then add the chopped sweet potato and 1 tsp of the chili flakes. Cook for 1 min.

2 Pour in the veg stock along with some seasoning, bring to the boil then reduce to a simmer and gently cook for 15 mins.

3 Toss the spiralized sweet potato with the remaining oil and chilli flakes on a large baking sheet. Spread the potato out so it cooks evenly then roast, turning halfway, for 20 mins until softened, caramelized and crisping at the edges. Keep checking after 15 mins to make sure they aren't burning.

4 After 15 mins check that the sweet potato is tender, then blitz the soup with the lime zest and juice until completely smooth. Taste for seasoning, then spoon into bowls and top with the roasted sweet potato and some sour cream or coconut yoghurt, if you like.

PER SERVING 193 kcals, fat 6g, sat fat 4g, carbs 30g, sugars 14g, fibre 5g, protein 3g, salt 0.4g

Alkalizing green soup

This kale, courgette, ginger and turmeric soup is super-healthy and full of nutrients.

🕐 TAKES 35 mins   🍳 SERVES 2

- 1 tbsp sunflower oil
- 2 garlic cloves, sliced
- thumb-sized piece ginger, sliced
- ½ tsp ground coriander and turmeric
- pinch of pink Himalayan salt
- 200g courgettes, roughly sliced
- 500ml vegetable stock
- 85g broccoli
- 100g kale, chopped
- zest and juice of 1 lime
- small pack of parsley, roughly chopped, reserving a few whole leaves to serve

1 Heat the oil in a deep pan, add the garlic, ginger, coriander, turmeric and salt, fry on a medium heat for 2 mins, then add 3 tbsp water to give a bit more moisture to the spices.

2 Add the courgettes, making sure you mix well to coat the slices in all the spices, and continue cooking for 3 mins. Add 400ml stock and leave to simmer for 3 mins.

3 Add the broccoli, kale and lime juice with the rest of the stock. Leave to cook again for another 3–4 mins until all the vegetables are soft.

4 Take off the heat and add the chopped parsley. Pour everything into a blender and blend on high speed until smooth. It will be a beautiful green with bits of dark speckled through (which is the kale). Garnish with lime zest and reserved parsley leaves.

PER SERVING 182 kcals, fat 8g, sat fat 1g, carbs 14g, sugars 4g, fibre 5g, protein 10g, salt 0.7g

Three bean veggie chilli

High in fibre and vitamin C, this vegan chilli is low fat and contains all of your five-a-day. Why not make double and freeze the rest?

🕐 TAKES 1 hr 10 mins　　🍽 SERVES 4

- 1 tbsp olive oil
- 2 red onions, ends trimmed and spiralized into flat noodles, any very long strands cut in half
- 2 mixed peppers, deseeded and chopped
- 2 fat garlic cloves, chopped
- 1 red chilli, finely chopped
- 1 tsp cayenne, ground cumin and dried oregano
- 500g carton passata
- 2 x 400g cans mixed beans, drained and rinsed
- 1 large butternut squash, peeled, ends trimmed, cut into half widthways and spiralized into thin noodles, any very long strands cut in half

1 Heat the oil in a large saucepan over a low to medium heat. Add the onion and peppers and cook gently for 10 mins. Increase the heat and stir in the garlic, chilli and spices. Cook for 1–2 mins until fragrant.

2 Pour in the passata, 200ml water, the mixed beans and some seasoning. Bring to the boil then reduce to a simmer and bubble away for 30 mins.

3 Stir in the spiralized butternut with a splash of water if the chilli is dry, taste for seasoning and continue to cook for 10 mins until the sauce is thick and the squash is tender.

PER SERVING 225 kcals, fat 4g, sat fat 1g, carbs 34g, sugars 24g, fibre 12g, protein 7g, salt 0.1g

Chicken, carrot & sweetcorn ramen

A play on the soothing Japanese noodle soup, this chicken ramen uses carrot noodles.

🕐 TAKES 45 mins plus marinating 📖 SERVES 4

- 4 boneless, skinless chicken breasts, about 500g, thinly sliced
- 2 tsp sesame oil
- 4 garlic cloves, 2 cloves crushed, the other 2 left whole
- 4 tbsp light soy sauce
- 1 litre good-quality chicken stock
- thumb-sized piece of ginger, cut into 4 slices
- 1 red chilli, thinly sliced, deseeded if you like
- 1 tbsp groundnut oil
- 1 tbsp mirin
- 325g can sweetcorn, drained
- 4 carrots (about 450g), ends trimmed and spiralized into thin noodles, any very long strands cut in half
- 4 spring onions, thinly sliced on a diagonal

1 Toss the sliced chicken in a large bowl with the sesame oil, crushed garlic, 2 tbsp of soy and a generous grind of black pepper. Leave to marinate for 20 mins if you have time.

2 Pour the stock along with 300ml water, ginger, chilli and remaining garlic cloves into a large saucepan. Bring to the boil then reduce the heat and simmer for 10 mins to allow the aromatics to infuse.

3 Meanwhile, heat the groundnut in a large frying pan over a medium heat. Add the chicken and fry for 5–7 mins until cooked through.

4 Add the remaining soy sauce, mirin, sweetcorn and spiralized carrot to the soup. Simmer for 2 mins then tip in the fried chicken and cook for a further 1–2 mins until the carrot is tender. Taste for seasoning then spoon into bowls and top with the spring onion.

PER SERVING 336 kcals, fat 8g, sat fat 2g, carbs 22g, sugars 14g, fibre 7g, protein 41g, salt 3g

Moroccan vegetable stew

If you'd prefer to make a vegan version, top with coconut yoghurt.

🕐 TAKES 1 hour 5 mins   🕒 SERVES 4

- 1 tbsp cold-pressed rapeseed oil
- 1 medium onion, peeled and finely sliced
- 2 thin leeks, trimmed and cut into thick slices
- 2 large garlic cloves, peeled and finely sliced
- 2 tsp ground coriander and cumin
- ½ tsp dried chilli flakes
- ¼ tsp ground cinnamon
- 400g can chopped tomatoes
- mixed peppers, deseeded and cut into chunks
- 400g can chickpeas, drained and rinsed
- 100g dried split red lentils
- 375g sweet potatoes, peeled and cut into chunks
- juice of 1 large orange plus peel, thickly sliced
- 50g mixed nuts, roughly chopped
- fresh coriander and natural yoghurt, to serve (optional)

1 Heat the oil in a large flameproof casserole or saucepan and gently fry the onion and leeks for 10–15 mins until well softened, stirring occasionally. Add the garlic and cook for 2 mins more.

2 Stir in the ground coriander, cumin, chilli and cinnamon. Cook for 2 mins, stirring occasionally. Add the chopped tomatoes, peppers, chickpeas, lentils, sweet potatoes, orange peel and juice, half the nuts and 400ml water and bring to a simmer. Cook for 15 mins, adding a splash of water if the stew looks too dry, and stir occasionally until the potatoes are softened but not breaking apart. Season to taste.

3 Remove the pan from the heat and ladle the stew into bowls. Scatter with the remaining nuts and top with chopped coriander and yoghurt, if using.

PER SERVING 482 kcals, fat 14g, sat fat 2g, carbs 63g, sugars 26g, fibre 15g, protein 18g, salt 0.6g

Spiralized Singapore noodles

Swapping noodles for vegetables brings this delicious, spicy dish up to four of your five-a-day.

🕐 TAKES 35 mins   📖 SERVES 2

- 2 tsp coconut or vegetable oil
- thumb-sized piece ginger, chopped
- 1 fat red chilli, ½ finely chopped, ½ thinly sliced into rings
- 2 fat garlic cloves, crushed
- 6 spring onions, finely sliced
- 1½ tbsp curry powder
- 2 tbsp soy sauce
- 1 tbsp teriyaki sauce
- 150g pack raw prawns, roughly chopped
- 100g cooked ham, shredded
- 1 large mooli (daikon radish), ends trimmed and spiralized into thin noodles
- 2 courgettes or 3 carrots, ends trimmed and spiralized into thick noodles
- 2 large handfuls of beansprouts, coriander and lime wedges, to serve

1 Heat the oil in a wok over a high heat. When hot, add the ginger, chopped chilli, garlic and spring onions and stir-fry for 30 secs–1 min until just softened. Add the curry powder, soy sauce, teriyaki sauce, prawns and ham and cook for another 2 mins, until the prawns turn pink.

2 Add the vegetable noodles and beansprouts, stir around the pan for 1 min more until the noodles have softened a little but still have a nice bite – don't cook for too long or they will turn watery. Serve scattered with coriander and the sliced chilli, with lime wedges on the side.

PER SERVING 298 kcals, fat 7g, sat fat 3g, carbs 25g, sugar 21g, fibre 10g, protein 29g, salt 4.4g

Butternut mac 'n' cheese

All of the comfort of mac n cheese without the pasta. Use this recipe as a base and experiment with other vegetable noodles.

🕐 TAKES 1 hr   🕐 SERVES 6

- 50g butter
- 50g plain flour
- 1 tsp mustard powder
- 600ml milk
- 250g extra mature Cheddar, grated
- 2 medium butternut squash (about 900g each), peeled, ends trimmed, halved and spiralized into thick noodles
- 30g Parmesan, grated
- 30g dried breadcrumbs
- 2 sprigs of thyme, leaves picked and finely chopped
- ½ tsp cayenne

1 Heat oven to 200C/180C fan/gas 6. Melt the butter in a medium saucepan over a medium heat. Once melted stir in the flour and mustard powder. Mix to a smooth paste and cook, stirring for 1 min.

2 Gradually whisk in the milk until you have a smooth sauce. Simmer for 3–4 mins, whisking constantly until the sauce has thickened. Remove the pan from the heat and stir in the Cheddar. Once melted, taste for seasoning, I like to add a generous grind of black pepper.

3 Put the butternut noodles into a large bowl and pour over the cheese sauce, mixing well so that every strand is coated in the sauce then tip into a large ovenproof dish (about 25 x 30cm). In a small bowl mix together the Parmesan, breadcrumbs, thyme and cayenne.

4 Scatter the breadcrumb mixture over the top of the butternut then bake for 20–25 mins until bubbling, crisp and golden.

PER SERVING 431 kcals, fat 27g, sat fat 17g, carbs 27g, sugar 11g, fibre 3g, protein 18g, salt 1.2g

Courgette vongole

Clams are in season from September to February in the UK. Make the most of them in this fresh twist on an Italian classic.

🕐 TAKES 35 mins   📖 SERVES 2

- 500g fresh clams, scrubbed
- 2 tbsp extra virgin olive oil
- 1 fat garlic clove, finely chopped
- 1 small red chilli, finely chopped
- 5 cherry tomatoes, halved
- ½ small pack parsley, stalks and leaves chopped
- 100ml dry white wine
- 2 large courgettes, ends trimmed and spiralized into thin noodles

1 Pick through the clams, discarding any with broken shells and any that stay open when you try to close them. Wash the clams in 2 changes of water.

2 Heat a sauté pan, with a lid, over a high heat. Stirring constantly, add the oil, garlic, chilli, tomatoes and parsley stalks and cook for 1-2 mins until the garlic is golden (watch it as you don't want it to burn). Pour over the wine, followed by the clams.

3 Pop the lid on the pan and cook the clams for 3 mins, until the majority have opened. Tip in the courgetti, place the lid back on and turn off the heat. Give everything a good shake, then leave to sit for a minute or so that the courgetti softens slightly.

4 Get rid of any clams that haven't opened, stir in the parsley, season to taste, spoon into bowls and serve immediately.

PER SERVING 275 kcals, fat 13g, sat fat 2g, carbs 9g, sugar 4g, fibre 3g, protein 20g, salt 1.9g

Courgetti turkey Bolognese

Turkey mince and courgetti are a lighter and delicious alternative that transform this much-loved family staple.

TAKES 1 hr 15 mins   SERVES 4

- 2 tbsp olive oil
- 500g turkey mince (thigh or breast)
- 1 large onion, finely chopped
- 1 garlic clove, crushed
- 2 large carrots, peeled and diced
- 150g pack button mushrooms, roughly chopped
- 1 tbsp tomato purée
- 2 x 400g cans chopped tomatoes
- 2 chicken stock cubes
- 1 tbsp soy sauce
- 4 large courgettes, ends trimmed and spiralized into thick noodles
- grated pecorino to serve
- handful basil leaves

1 Heat 1 tbsp of the olive oil in a large saucepan and add the turkey mince. Fry until browned, then scoop into a bowl and set aside.

2 Add the onion to the pan and cook on a low heat for 8–10 mins until tender. Add the garlic, cook for 1 min or so, followed by the carrots and the mushrooms. Cook for about 3 mins, until softened. Tip the turkey mince back into the pan, add the tomato purée, give everything a quick stir and tip in the chopped tomatoes. Fill 1 can with water and pour into the pan. Crumble over the chicken stock cubes and bring to the boil. Once boiling, lower the heat and simmer for about 1 hr, until the sauce has thickened and the veg is tender.

3 When the Bolognese is nearly ready, stir through the soy sauce and some seasoning. Heat a large frying pan with the remaining 1 tbsp olive oil and add your courgetti. Cook until slightly softened, for 2–3 mins. Season with salt and serve topped with the turkey Bolognese, grated cheese and basil leaves.

PER SERVING 326 kcals, fat 8g, sat fat 1g, carbs 20g, sugar 17g, fibre 8g, protein 39g, salt 2.6g

Toasted hazelnut & parsnip pappardelle

A toasted hazelnut ragout and poached egg add indulgence to this gluten-free dish.

🕐 TAKES 30 mins   ◔ SERVES 3

- 1 tbsp white wine vinegar
- 1 tbsp hazelnut oil
- 4 large parsnips (about 700g), peeled, ends trimmed and spiralized into flat noodles
- 50g blanched hazelnuts, toasted and chopped
- 100ml single cream
- 3 large eggs, the fresher the better
- ½ small pack of oregano, leaves picked
- Parmesan, to serve (optional)

1 Fill a large saucepan with cold water. Add the vinegar and bring to the boil.

2 While the water is boiling, heat the oil in a frying pan over a medium heat. Tip in the spiralized parsnip and cook for 3–4 mins, stirring occasionally until nearly tender. Stir in the toasted hazelnuts, cream and some seasoning then reduce the heat to low and leave to gently tick over while you poach the eggs.

3 Lower the heat so that the water is simmering rather than boiling then crack in the eggs. Poach for 2 mins then lift out with a slotted spoon and drain on kitchen paper.

4 If the sauce is dry add a splash of water then stir in the oregano and taste for seasoning. Divide between plates and top each portion with a poached egg and a good grind of black pepper. Serve with Parmesan at the table, if you like.

PER SERVING 471 kcals, fat 28g, sat fat 7g, carbs 33g, sugar 13g, fibre 10g, protein 16g, salt 0.3g

Lentil ragu with courgetti

This ragu freezes well in individual portions, so is a great one to have to hand for a quick go-to dinner.

🕐 TAKES 55 mins 🫐 SERVES 8

- 2 tbsp rapeseed oil, plus 1 tsp
- 3 celery sticks, chopped
- 2 carrots, chopped
- 4 garlic cloves, chopped
- 2 onions, finely chopped
- 140g button mushrooms from a 280g pack, quartered
- 500g pack dried red lentils
- 500g pack passata
- 1 litre reduced-salt vegetable stock
- 1 tsp dried oregano
- 2 tbsp balsamic vinegar
- 3-4 large courgettes, ends trimmed and spiralized into thin noodles

1 Heat the 2 tbsp oil in a large sauté pan. Add the celery, carrots, garlic and onions, and fry for 4–5 mins over a high heat to soften and start to colour. Add the mushrooms and fry for 2 mins more.

2 Stir in the lentils, passata, stock, oregano and balsamic vinegar. Cover the pan and leave to simmer for 30 mins until the lentils are tender and pulpy. Check occasionally and stir to make sure the mixture isn't sticking to the bottom of the pan; if it does, add a drop of water.

3 To serve, heat the remaining oil in a separate frying pan, add the courgetti and stir-fry briefly to soften and warm through. Serve half the ragu with the courgetti and chill the rest to eat on another day.

PER SERVING 578 kcals, fat 7g, sat fat 1g, carbs 87g, sugar 19g, fibre 14g, protein 35g, salt 0.2g

Sticky pork noodles

Five spice, soy and honey make up the sticky marinade for these low-fat pork noodles.

🕐 TAKES 40 mins   📋 SERVES 4 plus marinating

- 400g pork tenderloin fillet, thinly sliced
- 1 tbsp groundnut or sunflower oil
- 2 fat garlic cloves, thinly sliced
- thumb-sized piece of ginger, peeled and sliced into matchsticks
- 1 red chilli, deseeded and thinly sliced into matchsticks
- 200g okra, cut in half lengthways
- 1 large mooli, ends trimmed and spiralized into thin noodles
- 2 large carrots, ends trimmed and spiralized into thin noodles
- 300g pak choi, leaves separated
- 4 spring onions, thinly sliced on the diagonal

FOR THE MARINADE
- 1 tsp five spice
- 4 tbsp low-sodium soy sauce
- 2 tbsp honey

1 Mix all the marinade ingredients together in a large bowl. Stir in the sliced pork, cover and leave to marinate for 30 mins in the fridge, if you have time.

2 Heat the oil in a wok or a large frying pan over a high heat. Once searing add the garlic, ginger and chilli. Fry, stirring frequently, for 1–2 mins until fragrant. Using a slotted spoon, add the pork, reserving the marinade, and cook for a further 2 mins, until browned.

3 Tip in the okra, mooli and carrots and fry for 3 mins then stir in the pak choi and pour over the rest of the marinade. Cook for a further 1–2 mins until the pak choi has wilted, the pork and veg are tender and everything is coated in the sticky sauce.

4 Divide between plates and top with the sliced spring onion to serve.

PER SERVING 269 kcals, fat 8g, sat fat 2g, carbs 20g, sugar 19g, fibre 7g, protein 26g, salt 2g

Kale & walnut pesto courgetti

Kale pesto is a great way to sneak extra veg into your diet. Kids will love this simple vegan meal.

🕐 TAKES 30 mins 🥧 SERVES 6

- 70g walnuts
- 200g bag of kale, stems removed
- 2 red chillies, deseeded if you like
- 1 preserved lemon, pulp discarded
- juice of ½ lemon
- 2 garlic cloves, chopped
- small pack basil, leaves only
- 110ml extra virgin olive oil
- 7 large courgettes (about 1300g), ends trimmed and spiralized into thick noodles

1 Heat oven to 180C/160C fan/gas 4. Spread the walnuts out on a baking tray and roast for 10 mins until golden brown.

2 While the nuts are toasting, bring a large pan of water to the boil. Tip in the kale leaves, cook for 30 seconds then remove with a slotted spoon and immediately plunge into a bowl of ice-cold water. Reserve the water for later. Once cold, drain and squeeze out any moisture in a clean kitchen towel.

3 Put the kale, walnuts, red chillies, preserved lemon, lemon juice, garlic, basil and olive oil into a food processor and blitz until smooth. Try the pesto and season to taste.

4 Bring the pan of water back to the boil then drop in the courgetti. Cook for 1 min then drain, reserving a little water. Return to the pan and mix with enough pesto to generously coat the noodles, adding a little water to get your desired thickness, if necessary. Any left-over pesto will keep covered in the fridge for 3 days.

PER SERVING 319 kcals, fat 28g, sat fat 4g, carbs 8g, sugar 4g, fibre 3g, protein 8g, salt 0g

Summer courgetti & meatballs

Roast tomatoes with whole garlic cloves then squeeze the garlic out of their skins to make these delicious meatballs in a creamy garlicky sauce.

🕐 TAKES 40 mins 📋 SERVES 4

- 400g pork mince
- 4 garlic cloves, 2 crushed, 2 left whole and unpeeled
- 2 tbsp olive oil, plus extra for frying
- 400g cherry tomatoes
- 4 tbsp half-fat crème fraîche
- zest of 1 lemon
- 4 fat courgettes, ends trimmed and spiralized into thin noodles
- 50g pine nuts, toasted, to serve
- large handful of basil, to serve
- Parmesan shavings, to serve (optional)

1 Heat oven to 200C/180C fan/gas 6. Put the mince in a bowl, season well and add the crushed garlic. Mix together with your hands, then shape into small meatballs. Heat 1 tbsp of the oil in a large frying pan, add the meatballs and fry for 10–15 mins until golden brown. Meanwhile, toss the tomatoes in a roasting tin with the whole garlic cloves, remaining oil and some seasoning. Roast for 15 mins.

2 Once cooked, tip the meatballs into the roasting tin with the tomatoes, fish out the garlic and set aside, then cover the tin with foil to keep warm.

3 Wash the frying pan. Heat another 1 tbsp oil in the pan, squeeze the garlic cloves from their skins into the pan and mash with a fork. When sizzling, add the crème fraîche, lemon zest and some seasoning. Add the courgetti and toss in the pan for 30 secs until warmed through. Remove the pan from the heat, and tip in the meatballs, tomatoes and any juices from the tin. Mix together and scatter with pine nuts, basil and Parmesan, if you like.

PER SERVING 389 kcals, fat 28g, sat fat 7g, carbs 7g, sugar 6g, fibre 4g, protein 26g, salt 0.2g

Chicken satay stir-fry

If you don't like peanut butter substitute for any nut butter, such as cashew or almond in this easy chicken stir-fry with sweet potato noodles.

🕐 TAKES 40 mins   🕐 SERVES 2

- 1 tbsp coconut oil
- 2 skinless and boneless chicken breasts (about 300g) cut into thin slices
- 200ml coconut milk
- 2 medium sweet potatoes (about 350g), peeled, ends trimmed and spiralized into thin noodles
- 200g mixed pack baby corn and mangetout, corn cut in half lengthways

FOR THE SATAY SAUCE
- small piece of ginger, peeled and finely grated
- 1 garlic clove, finely grated
- 1 tbsp soy sauce
- 2 tbsp peanut butter
- 1 tsp chilli flakes
- zest and juice of ½ lime

1 Mix together all the ingredients for the satay sauce in a small bowl and set aside.
2 Heat the oil in a wok or large frying pan over a high heat. Season the chicken then fry for 5 mins until just cooked through and golden. Remove with a slotted spoon and transfer to a plate.
3 Tip the satay sauce into the pan, let it sizzle for 1 min then pour in the coconut milk. Once bubbling stir in the sweet potato noodles and reduce the heat. Simmer gently for 4 mins.
4 Add the corn, mangetout and chicken back to the pan. Simmer for a further 3–4 mins until the noodles are tender, then divide between plates.

PER SERVING 629 kcals, fat 29g, sat fat 21g, carbs 43g, sugar 20g, fibre 9g, protein 45g, salt 1.6g

Parma ham & basil courgetti

Make your own delicious tomato and mascarpone sauce to go with courgetti and crispy Parma ham.

🕐 TAKES 45 mins   🔥 SERVES 2

- 1 tbsp olive oil
- 1 shallot, finely chopped
- 1 garlic clove, crushed
- 400g can of chopped tomatoes
- ½ tbsp balsamic vinegar
- 4 slices of Parma ham, roughly torn
- 2 tbsp mascarpone
- 2 courgettes, ends trimmed and spiralized into thin noodles
- ½ small pack of basil, leaves roughly torn

1 Heat the oil in a sauté pan over a low heat. Add the shallot and a pinch of salt and cook gently for 8 mins until softened but not coloured. Stir in the garlic clove and cook for a further minute then tip in the chopped tomatoes and balsamic vinegar. Bring the sauce up to the boil then simmer away for 20 mins.

2 Meanwhile, dry-fry the Parma ham in a separate frying pan until crisp then set aside on a plate.

3 Taste the sauce and adjust the seasoning then stir in the mascarpone. Once bubbling away, stir in the courgetti and cook for 1–2 mins until the noodles are just tender. Divide the pasta and sauce between bowls then top with the crisp ham and basil.

PER SERVING 383 kcals, fat 28g, sat fat 14g, carbs 13g, sugar 12g, fibre 4g, protein 17g, salt 1.8g

Bacon & mushroom celeriac pasta

High in fibre, celeriac is used in place of pasta in this creamy winter warmer.

🕐 TAKES 35 mins   🥧 SERVES 4

- 1 tsp olive oil
- 150g smoked bacon lardons
- 250g pack chestnut mushrooms, sliced
- 2 large celeriac (about 900g each), peeled, ends trimmed and spiralized into thick noodles
- 2 garlic cloves, crushed
- 200ml tub of crème fraiche
- zest of 1 lemon
- ½ small pack of parsley, chopped

1. In a large frying or sauté pan heat the oil over a medium to high heat. Add the bacon, mushrooms and celeriac noodles to the pan and fry, stirring frequently, for 5 mins, until the bacon is crisp.
2. Decrease the heat slightly and stir in the garlic. Cook for 1–2 mins until the noodles are tender then spoon in the crème fraiche and lemon zest. Give everything a good stir so that it is coated in the sauce and season – a generous grind of black pepper here is welcome. Divide among bowls and scatter over the chopped parsley.

PER SERVING 425 kcals, fat 30g, sat fat 16g, carbs 12g, sugar 9g, fibre 23g, protein 15g, salt 2.1g

Carrot pad Thai

Carrot noodles add colour and sweetness to this punchy prawn pad Thai.

🕐 TAKES 35 mins 📖 SERVES 6

- 2 tbsp tamarind paste mixed with 1 tbsp water
- 2 tbsp fish sauce
- 2 tbsp palm sugar or soft brown sugar
- 1 tbsp groundnut or sunflower oil
- 1 garlic clove, thinly sliced
- 1 red chilli, thinly sliced
- 3 large carrots (about 350g), ends trimmed and spiralized into thin noodles
- 150g pack raw king prawns
- 2 large eggs, beaten
- 200g beansprouts
- handful of chives, finely chopped
- 20g roasted peanuts, roughly chopped
- 1 lime, cut into wedges to serve

1 Mix together the tamarind, fish sauce and sugar together in a small bowl, stirring until the sugar dissolves, then set aside.

2 Heat the oil in a wok or large frying pan over a high heat. Once searing, add the garlic and chilli, stir-fry for 1 min then tip in the carrots and king prawns. Stir for for 1–2 mins, until the prawns have just turned pink.

3 Push everything to the side of the wok and pour in the eggs. Leave to set for 1 min then scramble. Once scrambled, tip in the beansprouts, mix everything together, then pour over the sauce.

4 Cook for a further minute or so until everything is heated through then give the pad Thai a final mix. Divide between bowls, top with the chopped chives and peanuts and serve with a lime wedge for squeezing.

PER SERVING 458 kcals, fat 17g, sat fat 4g, carbs 44g, sugar 31g, fibre 8g, protein 29g, salt 3.9g

Courgetti puttanesca

An Italian store-cupboard staple, this pasta sauce is packed full of bold flavours.

🕐 TAKES 30 mins   📋 SERVES 4

- 3 tbsp olive oil
- 6 anchovies, chopped
- 2 fat garlic cloves, crushed
- ½–1 tsp chilli flakes, depending on your liking
- 400g can chopped tomatoes
- 100g black olives, stoned and roughly chopped
- 1 tbsp capers, rinsed and roughly chopped
- 4 large courgettes, ends trimmed and spiralized into thin noodles
- ½ small pack of basil, leaves picked and torn (optional)

1 Heat the oil in a large sauté pan over a medium heat. Add the anchovies and cook for 3 mins, pressing down with the back of a spoon to melt the anchovies into the oil. Stir in the garlic and chilli flakes and cook for 1–2 mins until sizzling and fragrant.

2 Tip in the chopped tomatoes, olives and capers. Stirring occasionally, let the sauce bubble away for 8 mins until thickened slightly, then add the courgetti. Mix well so that each strand is covered in the sauce and cook for a further 2–3 mins until tender.

3 Taste for seasoning then scatter over the basil leaves, if using. Serve sharing style, plonked in the middle of the table for people to help themselves.

PER SERVING 201 kcals, fat 14g, sat fat 2g, carbs 9g, sugar 7g, fibre 6g, protein 6g, salt 1.3g

Sweet potato Genovese

Taking the essence of a classic pasta Genovese with potatoes and pesto, we are turning it on its head using sweet potato as the noodles in this herby dish.

🕐 TAKES 35 mins   🍽 SERVES 2

- 2 medium sweet potatoes (about 400g), peeled, ends trimmed and spiralized into thick noodles
- 200g fine green beans, trimmed and cut in half

FOR THE PESTO
- 1 small pack of basil
- 1 small garlic clove
- zest and juice of ½ lemon
- 30g pecorino cheese, grated, plus extra for serving
- 3 tbsp extra virgin olive oil

1 Blitz together the basil, garlic, lemon, pecorino and olive oil in a food processor and season to taste. Alternatively, you can make the pesto using a pestle and mortar, just remember to add the oil after the other ingredients have been ground.

2 Bring a medium saucepan of salted water to the boil. Once boiling drop in the sweet potato noodles and simmer gently for 2 mins then add the green beans. Simmer for 1–2 mins more until the beans are cooked and the potato is tender then drain, reserving a little of the water.

3 Return the sweet potato and green beans to the pan and stir through the pesto. You want the sauce to coat every noodle strand, if too thick, loosen with some of the reserved water.

4 Divide between bowls, season with a good grinding of black pepper and serve with extra pecorino, for grating.

PER SERVING 326 kcals, fat 22g, sat fat 3g, carbs 17g, sugar 13g, fibre 7g, protein 11g, salt 1.8g

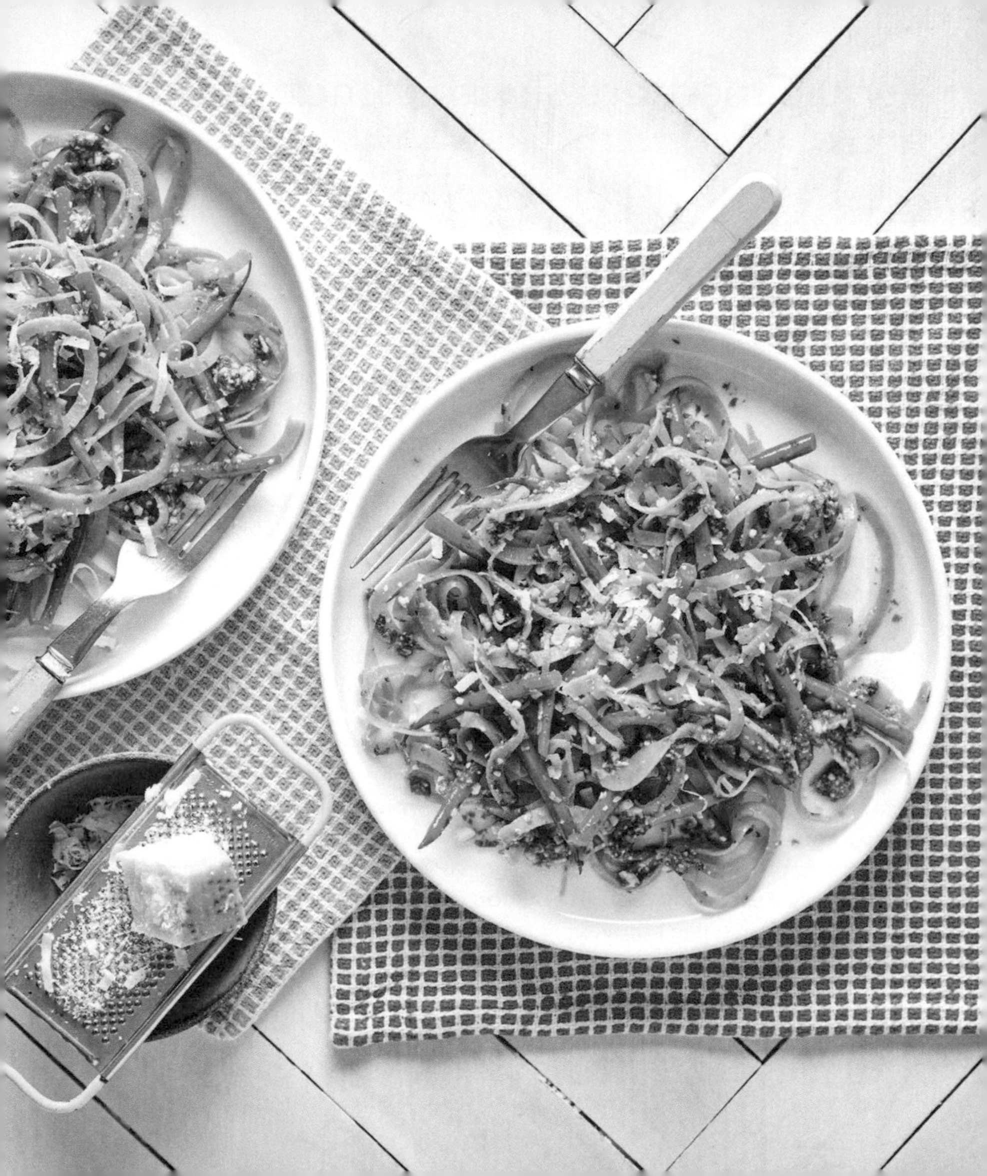

Veggie meatballs with tomato courgetti

These meatballs use ground almonds rather than breadcrumbs to increase the protein content and keep them gluten-free.

🕐 TAKES 30 mins   🕒 SERVES 2

- 2 tsp rapeseed oil, plus extra for greasing
- 1 small onion, finely chopped
- 2 tsp balsamic vinegar
- 100g canned red kidney beans, rinsed and drained
- 1 tbsp beaten egg
- 1 tsp tomato purée
- 1 heaped tsp chilli powder
- ½ tsp ground coriander
- 15g ground almonds
- 40g cooked sweetcorn
- 2 tsp chopped thyme leaves
- 3 garlic cloves, finely chopped

FOR THE TOMATO COURGETTI

- 2 large tomatoes, chopped
- 1 tsp tomato purée
- 1 tsp balsamic vinegar
- 2 courgettes, ends trimmed and spiralized into thin noodles

1 Heat the oil in a large pan and fry the onion, stirring frequently, for 8 mins. Stir in the balsamic vinegar and cook for 2 mins more.

2 Meanwhile, put the beans in a bowl with the egg, tomato purée and spices and mash until smooth. Stir in the almonds and sweetcorn with the thyme, a third of the chopped garlic and the balsamic onions. Mix well and shape into about 8 balls the size of a walnut, and place on a baking tray lined with oiled baking parchment.

3 Heat oven to 220C/200C fan/gas 7 and bake the veggie meatballs for 15 mins until firm.

4 Meanwhile, put the tomatoes, tomato purée and balsamic vinegar in a pan and cook with 2–3 tbsp water until pulpy, then stir in the remaining garlic and courgetti. Turn off the heat as you want to warm the noodles rather than cook them. Serve with the veggie meatballs.

PER SERVING 258 kcals, fat 11g, sat fat 1g, carbs 24g, sugar 12g, fibre 9g, protein 12g, salt 0.7g

Sicilian cauliflower courgetti

Roasted cauliflower, saffron soaked currants and toasted pine nuts make this good-for-you vegan dish feel indulgent.

🕐 TAKES 35 mins   📋 SERVES 4

- 1 head of cauliflower, cut into small florets
- 2 tbsp olive oil
- 40g currants
- ½ tsp saffron
- zest and juice of 1 lemon
- 2 garlic cloves, crushed
- ½ tsp chilli flakes
- 3 large courgettes, ends trimmed and spiralized into thin noodles
- 30g pine nuts, toasted
- 1 tsp capers, rinsed
- 1 small pack parsley, chopped

1 Heat oven to 200C/180C fan/gas 6. Toss the cauliflower florets on a large baking tray with 1 tbsp of the oil and some seasoning. Roast in the oven for 20 mins until cooked and slightly charred.

2 In a small bowl mix the currants, saffron, lemon zest and juice with 50ml boiling water and leave to soak.

3 Once the cauliflower has been roasted heat the remaining oil in a sauté pan over a medium heat. Spoon in the garlic and chilli and cook for 1–2 mins until the garlic is golden. Add the courgetti, currant mix, pine nuts and capers. Cook for 2 mins until the courgetti is tender then stir in the roasted cauliflower and parsley. Season to taste.

PER SERVING 277 kcals, fat 16g, sat fat 2g, carbs 20g, sugar 17g, fibre 7g, protein 10g, salt 0.2g

Thai broccoli rice

Replacing rice with broccoli makes a colourful, healthy, quick vegetarian meal.

🕐 TAKES 35 mins   🍽 SERVES 4

- 100g salted peanuts
- 1 head of broccoli, cut into florets and the stem cut in half
- 2 tbsp olive oil
- 1 red onion, finely diced
- 1 garlic clove, crushed
- 1 tbsp grated ginger
- 1 medium red chilli, deseeded and finely diced
- ½ small red cabbage, shredded
- 1 red pepper, deseeded and sliced into strips
- small pack coriander, roughly chopped

FOR THE DRESSING

- zest and juice 1 lime
- 2 tbsp tamari
- ½ tbsp golden caster sugar
- 2 tbsp olive oil

1 Heat a frying pan over a medium heat and add the peanuts. Toast evenly, regularly shaking the pan, then remove and set aside.

2 Put the broccoli in a food processor and pulse until it looks like green couscous. Empty into a large bowl and set aside.

3 Heat the oil in a large frying pan and fry the onion, garlic, ginger and chilli until soft and aromatic. Add the broccoli rice to the pan and mix through, making sure everything is well coated. Sauté for 3–4 mins until al dente. Transfer to a large bowl and add the red cabbage, red pepper, half the coriander and half the toasted peanuts. Mix to combine.

4 Whisk all the dressing ingredients together until combined. Toss the dressing through the broccoli rice and transfer to a serving bowl or individual bowls. Top with the remaining coriander and peanuts.

PER SERVING 380 kcals, fat 26g, sat fat 4g, carbs 15g, sugar 13g, fibre 11g, protein 15g, salt 1.4g

Sausage, fennel & chilli butternut pasta

The butternut squash noodles add sweetness to this tasty spicy sausage pasta, a real family classic.

⏱ TAKES 30 mins   📂 SERVES 4

- 1 tbsp olive oil
- 400g pack of good-quality sausages (the best you can afford), meat squeezed from the skins
- 1 tsp chilli flakes
- 2 fat garlic cloves, crushed
- 2 tsp fennel seeds
- 2 tbsp tomato purée
- 250ml white wine
- 1 large butternut squash (about 1.2 kg), peeled, ends trimmed, halved and spiralized into thin noodles
- zest of 1 lemon
- ½ small pack of basil, leaves picked and torn, smaller leaves left whole
- Parmesan, to serve

1 Heat the oil in a large sauté pan over a medium heat. Add the sausage meat and fry, breaking the meat down with the back of a wooden spoon, until beginning to colour, then stir in the chilli, garlic and fennel seeds.

2 Continue to cook for 10 mins, until the meat is golden brown, crisp and beginning to caramelize. Stir in the tomato purée, cook for a minute to absolve the raw tomato taste then pour in the white wine. Once bubbling reduce the heat to a simmer, add the butternut squash noodles and cook gently for 5 mins until the noodles are tender, adding a splash of water if the sauce is looking too dry.

3 Taste for seasoning then stir in the lemon zest and basil leaves. Serve with a good grating of Parmesan cheese.

PER SERVING 539 kcals, fat 28g, sat fat 10g, carbs 43g, sugar 5g, fibre 4g, protein 17g, salt 1.3g

Bang bang chicken & vegetable noodles

For a vegetarian alternative, this dressing would also be great as a marinade for tofu.

🕐 TAKES 30 mins   🥧 SERVES 4

- 2 chicken breasts
- 4 courgettes, ends trimmed and spiralized into thick noodles
- 4 carrots, ends trimmed and spiralized into thick noodles
- 4 spring onions, finely sliced on an angle (save a few green parts to sprinkle on top)
- 150g beansprouts
- 180g frozen soya or edamame beans, defrosted

FOR THE DRESSING
- 4 tbsp smooth peanut butter
- 3 tbsp soy sauce
- 3 tbsp sweet chilli sauce
- 2 tbsp sesame oil
- zest and juice of 1 lime
- 50g honey-roasted peanuts, bashed with a rolling pin
- 1 red chilli, thinly sliced (optional)

1 Bring a large pan of seasoned water to a simmer, add the chicken breasts and lower the heat to a gentle simmer. Poach for 8–10 mins or until the chicken is cooked through – test by cutting in half through the thickest part. Transfer to a plate to cool.

2 Tip the spiralized courgette and carrots into a bowl with the spring onions, beansprouts and soya beans.

3 In another bowl make the dressing. Mash the peanut butter and soy sauce together to loosen the peanut butter, then whisk in the other ingredients and 1 tbsp water.

4 When the chicken is cool enough to handle, use two forks to shred it. Add to the vegetables, drizzle over the dressing and gently toss everything together until well coated. Transfer to a platter and scatter over the peanuts and chilli (if using). Leftovers will make a great packed lunch.

PER SERVING 440 kcals, fat 23g, sat fat 4g, carbs 22g, sugar 18g, fibre 9g, protein 31g, salt 2.4g

Index